Joan Scourfield   December 1977

Coronation Souvenirs

AND COMMEMORATIVES

Bilston Municipal Street Plaque.
Wolverhampton Art Gallery & Museums

The Coronation of King James I by an unknown German artist. 1603

Coronation Souvenirs

AND COMMEMORATIVES

DAVID RODGERS

LATIMER

First published in 1975 by
Latimer New Dimensions Limited
104 Earls Court Road, London W8 6EG

SBN 901539 33 3

Printed in Great Britain by The Anchor Press Ltd
and bound by Wm Brendon & Son Ltd
both of Tiptree, Essex

For M.V.L. and for C.E.M.

Contents

Acknowledgements

I should like to thank the following individuals, companies and institutions who have given me valuable time and advice in the preparation of this book.

The Local History Librarians of Birmingham and Wolverhampton.
Mr D. Taylor, Local History Librarian of Manchester.
Mr R. C. Jones of Liverpool Public Relations Department.
Mr S. Pittman of Birmingham Amenities and Recreation Department.
The Town Clerk of Sheffield.
Miss Lynne Bruton of The Forestry Commission.
Mr Steven Jackson of the Commemorative Collectors' Society.
Mr John Frost of the Newspaper Collectors' Club.
Miss Carol Edwards of Royal Doulton Limited.
Mr Bruce Tattersall of Wedgwood.
Miss B. N. Bailey of Royal Crown Derby.
Mr Ian Stuart and Mr. G. J. Luxton of Stuart Crystal.
Mr Tom Jones of Royal Brierley Crystal.
Mr D. Hutchinson of Thomas Goode and Co. Ltd.
Mr J. C. Cheetham of the Metal Box Company Limited.
Messrs. Sotheby & Co. Ltd.
Mr Hugh Wakefield and Miss Wendy Hefford of the Victoria and Albert Museum.
Mrs Phillippa Glanville of the London Museum.
Mr David Cordingly of Brighton Museum and Art Gallery.
Mr Stephen Gartin of the Harris Museum and Art Gallery, Preston.
Mr Christopher Allan of the Whitworth Art Gallery.
Mr Simon Hunt, Exeter Museum.
Dr Bernard Watney, Mr Michael Simpkin, Peter and Gill Jackson, Casimir Smith, Tom and Yvonne Jones, Mary Morris, John Davies and Roger Green.

My illegible manuscript was typed for me by Jan Thom who, together with the rest of my colleagues in Wolverhampton, had to put up with my extremely boring Coronation reminiscences for several months.

I should also like to thank all the Collectors, Public and Private, who have allowed objects to be reproduced.

D.E.R.

Introduction

The history of the British Coronation commemorative reflects not only the growth of manufacturing techniques and commercial commemoratives but the political, religious and social history of Great Britain. The decline in the power of the monarch and the rise of modern democracy are mirrored in the changing significance and distribution of souvenir items. Kings being mortal, reigns vary in length from the four years of James II to the sixty-four years of Victoria which means that the study of Coronation commemoratives cannot show the smooth development of style and society but rather sudden glimpses of temporary situations. For this reason considerable space has been given to development not immediately concerned with Coronations or Coronation years.

Although the first Coronation medal, that of Edward VI, appears in 1547, the majority of Royal commemoratives prior to 1761 cannot be safely attributed to specific Royal occasions. None the less they play an important role in the development of the Coronation commemorative tradition and have therefore been discussed.

It would be foolish to pretend that one could cover every Coronation item in a book of this length and without years of research. I have however, attempted to mention all the major categories of commemorative and souvenir in the hope that this will stimulate collectors and researchers alike.

Robert Southey wrote in 1807, 'There is, perhaps, no country in which the passion for collecting rarities is so prevalent as in England. . . . There is a popular notion, which has originated Heaven knows how, that a Queen Anne's farthing is worth £500; and some little while ago, an advertisement appeared in the newspapers offering one for sale at this price.'[1]

Southey would find little changed in 1974, the passion continues and the myths remain.

CHAPTER ONE Edward VI, the Early Stuarts and the Development of the Coronation Medal.

Writing to John Evelyn in July 1689, Samuel Pepys asks which portraits of the famous he should hang in his library. Evelyn had previously assisted the late Lord Chancellor Clarendon to amass his famous collection and was thus the acknowledged expert on such matters of historical taste. In his reply of the twelfth of August Evelyn recommends Pepys to consider a collection of medals rather than portraits; they are smaller and thus more easily displayed, they are doubtless less expensive and finally emphasis is placed on the sitter rather than the executor, a distinction which Evelyn unreservedly commends. Perhaps to convince Pepys of the social correctness of such a proceeding Evelyn cites Dr. Gale, Elias Ashmole and Clarendon's son as notable collectors.[2]

If Pepys acted on Evelyn's advice he would certainly have attempted to obtain the Coronation medal of Edward VI, the first Coronation commemorative.

The practice of issuing a Coronation medal began as a peculiarly British phenomenon which survived from the sixteenth to the twentieth century. Commemorative medals were first issued in Roman times and the practice was revived in renaissance Italy as a form of miniature portrait sculpture soon elevated to the highest artistry in the work of Pisanello and his successors. The fashion arrived in Tudor England by way of France and the Low Countries.

Edward VI's medal is the only Tudor Coronation commemorative. It is a large, clumsily cast medal, in gold or silver and was probably designed by Henry Basse, the Chief Engraver at the Royal Mint between 1544 and 1549(1).

The Latin inscription forms three concentric circles around the bust portrait of the young King. Translated it reads, 'Edward VI, by the Grace of God, King of England, France and Ireland, Defender of the Faith

The numbers in brackets refer to the illustrations.

and Supreme Head on Earth of the Church of England; crowned 20th February 1546 at the age of ten years.' The reverse has the same text in Hebrew and Greek and the word 'Lambhith' [Lambeth] where the Coronation took place.

It is tempting to speculate that Edward's medal may have had a particular political significance. After all there was no precedent and no subsequent Tudor Coronation medal. If instigated by Protector Somerset the medal might be seen as a record of intent implying no thoughts of usurpation; alternatively, the boy King was certainly precocious and able enough to have authorised the medal himself. In fact the medal appears to have had a primarily religious purpose. Only the previous year Henry VIII had issued a very similar medal probably also by Basse with the Latin inscription, 'Henry the Eighth, Defender of the Faith and Supreme Head of the Church of England and Ireland under Christ.' As with Edward's medal the inscription was repeated in Hebrew and Greek on the reverse. The use of these two learned ecclesiastical languages suggests that Henry's medal was intended as propaganda directly aimed at foreign clerics and as it is obviously the prototype for the Coronation medal it seems safe to assume that the latter was struck to stress the continuance of the Protestant Church of England at a time when the opportunities for a counter Reformation may have appeared strong.

Edward VI's medal although truly a Coronation commemorative can equally well be considered an item of Tudor political propaganda and it is not until the arrival on the English throne of the House of Stuart, over fifty years later, that a tradition of Coronation medals, unbroken until 1953, is established. James I of England and VI of Scotland was crowned for the second time on Monday July 25th 1603, his Coronation as King of Scotland having taken place in 1567 when he was one year old. James's progress through England was triumphant. He was greeted with general rejoicing by citizens and gentry alike and knighted several hundred of the latter during his journey from Edinburgh to London. His silver Coronation medal was designed for suspension from a ribbon and was intended for distribution to those present. The grandiloquent Latin inscription reads, 'James I, Caesar Augustus of Britain, Caesar the heir of the Caesars, presents this medal.' James abandoned his imperial pretensions after the first session of Parliament and settled for the title, King of Great Britain. His medal and the uniface medal of Anne, his Queen, began the tradition of the Coronation commemorative medal.

The obverse or front of Coronation medals shows only the portrait of the monarch, the reverse is frequently more revealing, particularly during the seventeenth century. The reverse of the gold Coronation medal of Charles I shows an arm brandishing a sword with the Latin inscription, 'Until peace be restored upon earth,' which refers simultaneously to the war against Spain and attempts to restore Charles' brother-in-law Frederick to the Bohemian Throne. The implicit suggestion of a speedy conclusion to both these problems was not to be fulfilled as domestic affairs were soon to occupy the King. Political motifs of more relevance to the English people were to appear on the medals of Charles II and William III.

The Restoration of the monarchy and the return of Charles II occasioned massive demonstrations of popular support. The King's entry into London was chronicled by Evelyn who reported, 'The wayes straw'd with flowers, the bells ringing, the streetes hung with tapissry, fountaines running with wine.'[3] Charles had been crowned in Scotland on New Year's Day 1651 and the negotiations over his return had been marked by the issuing of several propaganda medals, some intended as Royalist badges and some as rewards for personal services. Two official Coronation medals were struck by Thomas Simon. One, in gold and silver was for distribution among those present (2), the other, with a loop for suspension, was probably produced for the King's Household. The reverse of the latter bears an oak tree in full leaf supporting three crowns and the legend, *Already it Flourishes*, which refers to an earlier silver medal of 1660 the reverse of which shows the sun dispersing the clouds above a leafless oak tree with three crowns and the inscription, *At last it grows strong again*.

The propaganda medals produced for the Restoration are closely paralleled by those which heralded the arrival of William III twenty-eight years later. The official Coronation medal designed by George Bower has a double portrait obverse of William and Mary and a reverse of Perseus (William) rescuing Andromeda (England). A variant of this medal, for distribution to those present, has an obverse of two Bishops supporting the crown above the heads of the seated monarchs with the Latin inscription, 'Idolatry and slavery broken; religion, law and liberty restored.' A third medal in gold, silver or lead, has a reverse of Jupiter hurling a thunderbolt at Phaeton (James) who falls from his chariot. The Dutch produced several medals commemorating the Accession and Coronation the best known being that struck by Jan Smeltzing, portraying an Eagle (William) casting out a young bird (James Edward) from a nest containing two further eaglets (Mary and Anne).

William as Perseus and Jupiter may seem incongruous but when his stout and gouty sister-in-law, Anne, was crowned in 1702 Jan Boskam portrayed her as Pallas Athene hurling her thunderbolt at a double-headed, four-armed monster representing France and Spain on gold, silver and copper medals which also bore the splendid inscription, *She is the Vice-Regent of the Thunderer.*

With the Coronation of George I on the 20th October 1714 and the establishment of the Hanoverian dynasty the political significance of Coronation medals ceased, although that of George III bore the legend, *Rejoicing in the Fatherland*, thus emphasising the King's British birth and breeding in contrast with the Hanoverian background of his great grandfather and grandfather.

The Coronation of William IV was the last at which medals, costing £4,326 4s. 6d., were freely distributed. The practice of 'general distribution' had begun in the reign of James I and for several Coronations different medals were struck for the various categories of recipients. 'General distribution' is a misleading term, it seems likely that the Royal Household and servants received a medal in either gold or silver according to status, a further medal of gold or silver was distributed to the guests in the Abbey and a final distribution of silver or copper medals was made to the spectators in the Abbey yard. The practice of flinging the medals in the air like so much confetti was certainly established by the reign of Charles II. Pepys was disappointed in his efforts to obtain one, 'And a General Pardon also was read by the Lord Chancellor, and medals flung up and down by my Lord Cornwallis, of silver, but I could not come by any.'[4]

Mrs Dixon, at the Coronation of George III, was luckier, 'I need not tell you, that several Coronation medals in silver were thrown among the populace at the return of the procession. One of them was pitched into Mrs Dixon's lap as she sat upon a scaffold in Palace Yard. Some of gold were also thrown among the Peeresses within the Abbey, just after the King was crowned, but they thought it beneath their dignity to stoop and pick them up.'[5]

By George IV's Coronation the peeresses had become less proud and perhaps influenced by the King's own conduct as he sat on the throne 'nodding and winking . . . and sighing and making eyes at Lady Conynham . . .' they fought and scrummaged for the medals together with their peers. George's ostentatious disrepect for the ceremony was matched by

William IV's parsimonious disregard for it and if anything the great medal mêlée worsened. For reasons of decorum rather than thrift the ceremony was abandoned at Victoria's Coronation. Medals for public purchase were produced for the reigns of Victoria, Edward VII, George V, and George VI but the practice ceased in 1953 owing to the steady fall in public interest.

If William IV's Coronation saw the last of the old distributions, George IV's had seen the first of the new. Over 40 different medals were produced privately apart from the official medals by Thomas Wyon Jnr. (Even more medals were struck on behalf of Queen Caroline including those bearing such evocative titles as *Truth Triumphant, Malice Flees,* and *Britannia Welcomes*.) The towns of Manchester and Salford presented 25,697 medals to children. The practice of presenting commemorative medals was to spread to many other corporate and philanthropic bodies during the nineteenth century culminating in the striking of well over a hundred medals for the Coronation of King Edward VII in 1902.

Edward's Coronation was postponed from the 26th June to the 9th August owing to his illness and this resulted in two official issues, one with the correct and one with the incorrect date. Both were designed by De Saulles in gold, silver and bronze. The majority of the commercially produced medals had already been struck before June and most bear the incorrect date. Towns like Wolverhampton and Richmond could congratulate themselves on having chosen to show only the year of the Coronation and not the date (5). The enterprising Borough of Stoke Newington deleted June 26th with red enamel but most of the medals are misdated and correctly dated ones are rare. A particularly poignant medal was produced in silver by Elkington of Birmingham to the design of E. Fuchs and presented by the Countess of Warwick, a former mistress of the King, to the members of the Warwick Corporation.

Although the official medal was for sale Edward VII introduced medals for presentation to those attending the ceremony to be worn as campaign medals, a practice continued by George V who extended the range of recipients to include those in responsible public offices during Coronation Year.[6] The numbers of recorded medals produced had dropped to forty-two by the time of George V's Coronation, declined further to thirty-six for the proposed Coronation of Edward VIII, and were even fewer for that of George VI. The principal reasons for this decline were the rising prices and falling status of the medal and the strong growth of philately. William IV's medal had had an issue of 1,067 in gold and only 100 in bronzed copper; by Edward VII's time the gold medal cost £13 and the bronze 3s; George VI's large gold medal cost £52. 10s. and was produced in an issue of 267 whereas the bronze at 1s. 3d. numbered 70,433. The importance of the medal which in Victorian and Edwardian times had been associated with enterprise and achievement had, after two World Wars, become devalued and adults and children had turned to stamp collecting as a cheap and profitable hobby.[7] The lack of interest led the Coronation advisors to Elizabeth II to abandon the practice founded over 300 years before. With hindsight one can see that they were mistaken in assuming that official medals would not sell.

The potential demand had probably never been greater. The Exchange Control Act of 1947 had made it illegal to hold gold other than objects with a greater instrinsic value than that of the metal. This led to massive speculation in sovereigns and poorly produced gold medals, purchased as a hedge against inflation. A gold Coronation medal would have had an enormous if somewhat less than patriotic market.

As a substitute for an official medal the Coronation Crown (7) was produced[8] but the demand for presentation medals was such that officially approved obverse dies were struck by the Royal Mint and schoolchildren throughout the country received their medals after all.

From George V onwards the twentieth century Coronation medal seems to have been fated to fall into the hands of either speculators or schoolchildren. The importance of the medal declined from the reign of William IV, its significance emasculated by its availability. Mass produced commercial medals bearing loyal sentiments and a timely reminder of the particular benefactor (*Struck by the Makers of Elect Cocoa* is an example on a George VI medallion) further reduced the standing of the medal and badges, brooches and favours seemed less pompous patriotic accessories. Nonetheless the Coronation medal has an honourable history and without them we would have no mementoes of the Coronations of Edward VI and the early Stuarts.

CHAPTER TWO   The Later Stuarts

On April 30th 1649, John Evelyn records, 'Un-Kingship was proclaimed, and his Majesty's statues thrown down at St. Paul's Portico, and the Exchange.'[9] Such vandalism was to be common throughout the inter-regnum. Churches and homes alike were at the mercy of ecclesiastical, military, and civilian zealots. Images of monarchy and popery were particularly vulnerable. We shall probably never know whether royal commemoratives existed for the early Stuarts; if they did, they have not survived. Whether smashed as offensive symbols of oppression or as dangerous evidence of unfashionable sympathies, none now remain and with the exception of medals and prints, Coronation commemoratives date from the Restoration.

England under Cromwell achieved a great deal, particularly in the field of international expansion the fruits of which were to be reaped by later generations. The prosecution of a vigorous imperial policy meant higher taxes as did the maintenance of an unpopular standing army. The Puritanical elements in society prohibited village gatherings and ceremonies many of which were seen, perhaps rightly, to be of pagan origin. The maypoles were torn down, drinking and dancing were frowned upon and traditional pleasures were practised guiltily or not at all. By the time of Cromwell's death in October 1659 the regime was heartily unpopular. Writing of the Protector's funeral Evelyn says, 'it was the joyfullest funeral I ever saw; for there were none that cried but dogs, which the soldiers hooted away with a barbarous noise, drinking and taking tobacco in the streets as they went.'[10] Evelyn was of course a convinced Royalist but his report of the celebrations at the Restoration and Coronation of King Charles II is amply borne out by other observers. Not only in London were the streets running with wine, in Manchester 'the said conduits did run with pure Claret, which was freely drunk by all that could. . . . Bonfires being in every street . . . the Bells continued ringing night and day; some fireworks running upon cords the length of one hundred yards, and so backwards, with crackers in the ayre, which sport continued till almost midnight,' wrote William Heawood.[11] It seems likely that provincial Coronation celebrations began to take place on a much larger scale with the coming of the Restoration and continued to be celebrated in much the same way until the nineteenth century. They were not confined to Coronation year, but took place annually on the anniversary of the Coronation until a new monarch came to the throne thus assuming the character of a moveable feast. The form of the celebrations remained constant in Wolverhampton from 1701 until 1750 and consisted of roasting kids on bonfires (in 1727 four loads of coal cost 3s. and five kids 3d.) sack for the Constables and Gentry and ale for the townspeople.[12]

The Restoration, so eagerly awaited and joyfully celebrated, resulted in a demand for Royal commemoratives of the new King and his martyred father and the England of 1660 was far better able to provide them than the England of 1626. Two major categories of commemorative wares exist—glass and ceramics; and to trace the development of both it is necessary to return to the sixteenth century.

Although by 1661 heraldic and portrait enamelled glasses had been made in Venice for over 200 years and production had spread to South Germany by 1540, the English tradition of engraved glasses was far younger. In 1571 Giacomo Verzelini, a Venetian, arrived in London from Antwerp and on December 15th 1575 he received a monopoly to make English 'Venice' glasses for a period of 21 years. Verzelini employed Anthony de Lisle, a Frenchman, as an engraver, and the importance of Verzelini glass lies not so much in its manufacture, which had indeed already been established, though with little success, by John Carré, as in the quality and extent of the engraving which was a completely new departure for English glass. Less than ten Verzelini glasses are known, one of which, the Dier glass dated 1581, bears the Royal Arms (8). There is no suggestion that Verzelini, who died in 1606, produced any Royal commemorative but he was nonetheless responsible for the birth of an indigenous tradition of engraved heraldic glass and his Royal patronage soon made such glass fashionable. The first English allusion to engraved glasses appears in an inventory of Robert Dudley, Earl of Leicester dated 1588 which records 'eight graven dishes of glass about the brims,' and 'two graven bole glasses.'[13] It would seem quite likely given Dudley's close relationship with Queen Elizabeth that these were Verzelini glasses.

Verzelini's monopoly appears to have lapsed on his retirement in 1592 when Sir Jerome Bowes, a soldier by profession, was granted a twelve year monopoly. De Lisle probably engraved a Bowes glass of 1602 after which English engraved glass almost disappeared for sixty years. A rapid growth in demand for glass lead to concentration on more mundane productions; bottles replaced pottery and leather containers and glass panes replaced those of horn. Many luxury items that were produced must have perished during the Civil War and the Commonwealth when engraved glass was considered to be a relic of Royalty, a sinful extravagance and a challenge, by inference, to sobriety.

The Restoration brought about a marked change with the re-introduction of engraving from the Netherlands. Royalist families, anxious to drink the King's health were quick to commission glasses and 'nine King glasses' are recorded in the Household Accounts of Sir Richard Wynne of July 16th, 1665.[14] Three major examples of Restoration engraved glass survive. All three were probably made in London under the Duke of Buckingham's monopoly but engraved by Dutch artists. The Scudamore Flute is engraved with both the Royal Arms and the Scudamore Arms and was probably commissioned immediately after the King's return by John, Viscount Scudamore, 1601-71, an ardent Royalist. The Exeter Flute must also date from the early 1660's and is often described as a Coronation commemorative, in fact it seems more likely to have been commissioned for a dinner which the King attended (B). The final glass, the Royal Oak Goblet, is dated 1663 and was no doubt produced to commemorate the marriage of Charles and Catherine of Braganza. Despite the development of lead crystal glass by George Ravenscroft in the years following 1675, an invention that was to produce not only stronger, brighter and heavier glass but also to facilitate engraving, there are no recorded glasses commemorating the Coronation of King James II. There are very few for William and Mary (9) although an abundance of glasses commemorate the Battle of the Boyne on the 1st July 1690. The Boyne Glasses were to continue to be produced well into the eighteenth century in opposition to the Jacobite glasses glorifying the Old and Young Pretenders.

The introduction of wheel engraving during William's reign which greatly assisted the engraver's art is reflected in the few Anne Coronation glasses (10) and the many more produced to commemorate the Act of of Union in 1707.

Throughout the later Stuart period engraved glasses would have been specially commissioned either for presentation or for personal use. It is unlikely, therefore, that any glass can be considered simply as a Coronation commemorative piece although those produced immediately after the accession of a new monarch may well have been used to drink a health on Coronation Day.

Commemorative glass of the seventeenth and eighteenth centuries invariably takes the form of wine or ale glasses and, in a society where the drinking of healths was de rigeur and failure to drink to one's hosts' dedication could easily lead to bloodshed, commemorative glasses had considerable political significance. This was less so in the case of pottery, which also differed from glass in the market it catered for. In discussing the commemorative pottery of the later Stuarts the word 'Coronation' has to be used with caution. A few pieces, by reason of subject and date, may be considered as Coronation commemoratives but the vast majority of Royal pieces were produced throughout the reign of the monarch they represent and a significant number in the reigns of their successors.

Two categories of commemorative ceramics dominate the period, delft and slipware, the first imported and the latter indigenous. English majolica or English delft is essentially earthenware with a tin glaze which produces a white, non-porous surface eminently suitable for decoration. The origins of the technique and style are remarkably similar to those of English engraved glass.

Majolica had been produced in Italy from 1420 although the industry's greatest achievements date from after 1450. Although it was originally intended for utilitarian purposes, particularly drug jars, the Italians soon began to produce commemorative and heraldic decorations. The former were exclusively mementoes of domestic rejoicings, in particular marriages, rather than of affairs of state. Biblical and classical subjects abound but portrait plates, usually profile heads of women, were also produced in considerable numbers. Towards the end of the sixteenth century heraldic work was made on a large scale in Venice, already a centre for armorial glasses, and exported to southern Germany.

The Dutch production of majolica had undoubtedly been inspired by Italian example but the influence of the Far East, particularly China, played a decisive role over the decoration. The Dutch East India Company had proved to be considerably more successful than its British rival and throughout the sixteenth century had imported Chinese blue and white porcelain into the Netherlands. The long journey, frequent sea battles, and the fragile nature of this particular cargo meant that Chinese porcelain was a luxury article and the Dutch potters attempted to produce copies for middle class consumption.

In 1571 two Dutchmen, Jacob Janson and Jasper Andries petitioned Queen Elizabeth for permission to set up a pottery by the Thames thus introducing English delftware. By 1625 there was a pottery in Southwark. and by 1650 production had spread to Lambeth, Brislington and Bristol. English delftware was established and was to continue until the end of the eighteenth century.

Strangely enough there was no Dutch tradition of commemorative or portrait delftware and the English Royal chargers seem to be entirely independent of either Dutch or Italian influence although closer to the Italian 'piatto da pompa' or show plate in intention.

The earliest dated English delft plate is of the Tower of London in 1600 but there are no surviving Royal portrait chargers for James I and the few dated examples for Charles I are posthumous. The earliest, at Chequers, showing Charles and three of his children is dated 1653 and a full length portait plate sold at Sotheby's on the 5th March 1968 is dated 1658.

In 1934 R. H. Warren[15] listed dated pieces of Royal portrait delft and came up with the following figures, two Charles I, fifteen Charles II, four James II, sixty William, twenty William and Mary, five Mary, thirty Anne, ten George I and three George II. Although only concerned with dated examples Warren's list reveals the rise and fall of English delft and also the relative unpopularity of the Catholic James II which accounts for the few known pieces in any medium commemorating his reign.

The fashion for Royal portraits primarily on large dishes and chargers but also on bowls and mugs was, as has been mentioned, peculiarly English. The market for them seems likely to have been the less well off merchant class. The rich could afford Chinese porcelain although it was not to be fashionable until the 1690's, and ate off plate; the poor could afford no fripperies and ate off wood or coarse earthenware. The rich and middle classes alike however shared an interest in portraits of the famous and Celia Fiennes records of Lord Orford's house in the reign of William and Mary, that the hall was 'hung with pictures at full proportion of ye Royal family all in their Coronation Robes, from Charles the first to his Majesty with ye Queen also.' Landscapes were appreciated by only a few of the intelligentsia and as the poorer middle class could not afford paintings, what better than a portrait plate of a famous figure, and in a society which when not illiterate was certainly ill-read who was more famous than the monarch?

Such plates were not intended for eating off, plain whiteware or undecorated delft was suitable for that and the inland merchants who dealt in pottery might very well have purchased one of these brightly coloured plates when visiting their suppliers in London or Bristol.

Although there are possible exceptions, such plates would be mass-produced, on a limited scale, and not commissioned. Those with added personal initials (a practice incidentally, which had grown as a form of identifying one's expensive pewter) were almost certainly pre-decorated. Although not commissioned it is likely that earlier dated pieces for Charles II which include several fine wine cups, three of which are in the London Museum (14), were produced for a more refined market. The standard of decoration, so fine on these early pieces, deteriorates throughout the period of production until in the reign of George III it has wholly degenerated and is obviously intended for a much less sophisticated public.

The Glorious Revolution and the reign of William and Mary gave a new boost to delft. On the one hand many of the pieces were made in Holland and exported to England on the other the Queen's passion for China caused the widespread collecting of Chinese porcelain, which not unnaturally caused a boom in porcelain's poor relation, delft. The Queen's collection at Hampton Court was seen and admired by both Evelyn and Celia Fiennes and the consequences are brilliantly described by Defoe in 1724, 'The Queen [Mary] brought in the custom or humour, as I may call it, of furnishing houses with chinaware, which increased to a strange degree afterwards, piling their china upon the tops of cabinets, scritoires, and every chimney piece, to the tops of the ceilings, and even setting up shelves for their china-ware, where they wanted such places, till it became a grievance in the expense of it, and even injurious to their families and estates.'[16]

William was to continue to be recorded in delft as in glass throughout the reigns of the first two Georges as a symbol of Protestant ascendency. The production of Royal Oak dishes during the first half of the eighteenth century, however, probably commemorated kingship in general rather than Jacobite sympathies.

If delft may be seen as an example of international influence in the English pottery industry, an influence which in the case of China has persisted to the present day, then commemorative slipware can be seen as the last magnificent flowering of English traditional pottery.

Slipware which, very simply, is the name given to red earthenware decorated with applied lines and dots of a contrasting coloured, watered-down clay or slip was widely produced from the beginning of the seventeenth century but reached its apotheosis in the work of several Stafford-shire potters of the late seventeenth and early eighteenth centuries. The early ware is frequently found with geometric decoration and the sudden introduction of heraldic and portrait designs was probably an attempt by the traditional craftsmen to compete with the newly popular delft. Royal chargers in slipware are popularly connected with the name of Thomas Toft, best known for his splendid and huge chargers decorated with the Royal Arms (27). Fortunately the Staffordshire potters sign their work and we are thus able to identify George Taylor, William Taylor or Talor, and John Wright among others. The portrait dishes often with geometric arrangements of crowned heads are seldom inscribed with the Royal Cypher but usually dateable to a particular reign. Toft's Royal Arms dishes seem to date from the 1670's and Charles in the Royal Oak from 1660. Dishes showing Archbishop William Juxon and Charles II (25), although not necessarily produced in 1661, are among the very few Stuart items which we can call without hesitation Coronation com-memoratives. Slip, having a tendency to run, is usually found only on plates or chargers but a very rare jug by either George or William Taylor showing a full face portrait of the crowned Charles II was sold at Sotheby's on February 17th 1970.

A third ceramic development, which is to play a much greater part in the commemorative ware of the nineteenth century, impinges on this period. In seventeenth century and early eighteenth century stoneware can be found more Royal Cyphers, more busts and coats of arms than in either delftware or slipware yet, sadly, not one production can be considered commemorative. In 1672 John Dwight founded a pottery in Fulham for the production of saltglazed stoneware referred to in his patent of 1671 as pottery 'vulgarly called Cologne Ware.' Imports of tankards and bellarmines from Germany had grown during the second half of the seventeenth century and John Dwight was the first Englishman to take advantage of the enormous market for such products. The ware produced by the Fulham pottery and later by the South Staffordshire manufacturers was purely utilitarian and closely allied to the brewing trade. Bottles, tankards and jugs were the stock in trade of Dwight and his later competitors and for this reason many of their products bear either the Royal Cypher, Arms or Sovereign's bust, as an indication of capacity or excise mark (29).

Archeological work on the Fulham and South Staffordshire sites has discovered bellarmines and tankards bearing the Cyphers of William and Anne usually stamped into the clay although later products sometimes have applied marks. The excise stamp, which seems to have been applied by the factory rather than any outside body was loosely used particularly in Staffordshire, thus Anne's mark is often applied to tankards produced in the reign of George I and the Cypher of William is found upon the wares of Anne's reign. This loose usage eventually resulted in the Royal Cyphers and stamps being used for purely decorative purposes and we find examples not markedly different from the Fulham tankard with a relief bust portrait of Queen Anne, flanked by Beefeaters and Tudor roses and inscribed *Thomas Johnson 1727*[17] the Coronation year of George II.

Saltglaze stoneware was to survive the Stuart period and undergo a renaissance in the 1830's. Delft lingered on until the reign of George III when porcelain, far more akin to the products of China, was to predominate. Slipware as an unselfconcious production was to die during the eighteenth century and glass, combining the skills of science and art, was to outlast them all, surviving the industrial upheaval of the eighteenth and nineteenth centuries, into our own time.

CHAPTER THREE The First Three Georges

Between the Coronation of George I in 1714 and that of George III forty-seven years later two Royal figures dominate English commemorative wares, Bonnie Prince Charlie and Frederick the Great; the former in glass and the latter in pottery.

King George I, the Elector of Hanover, was, although popularly received as a Protestant, essentially the Whig candidate for the throne and many Tories, especially in the North, still looked for the return of a preferably Protestant Stuart to the throne of England. The alarms and excursions brought about by the King's accession are brilliantly evoked by Lady Mary Wortley-Montagu writing from York on August 3rd 1714: 'I went with my cousin today to see the King proclaimed, which was done, the Archbishop walking next the Lord Mayor, all the country gentry following with greater crowds of people than I believed to be in York, vast acclamations and the appearance of a general satisfaction, the Pretender afterwards dragged about the street, and burnt, ringing of bells, bonfires and illuminations, the mob crying liberty and property and long live King George. . . . This morning all the principal men of any figure took post for London, and we are alarmed with the fear of attempts from Scotland, though all Protestants here seem unanimous for the Hanover succession.'[18]

Some even feared a disturbance at the Coronation itself though, as Lady Dorchester remarked at the point in the ceremony when Recognition was required, 'Does the old fool think that anybody here will say "No" when there are so many drawn swords?'

As events proved, the Jacobite threat was abortive both in 1715 and 1745 and was treated with ever greater disdain throughout the eighteenth century. The growth of Jacobite commemoratives increased throughout the period, a paradox that can be explained by the growing complacency of the authorities. There are very few extant Jacobite glasses before 1745 and the greatest production took place between 1750 and 1770. Jacobite memorials were in greatest demand from the Tory political and drinking societies so it is hardly surprising that glass commemoratives greatly outnumber ceramic examples. Such few pieces as do exist include delft, Jackfield and other Shropshire productions after 1745 and a Longton Hall mug, transfer printed in Liverpool which must date from c.1760 when any real Stuart threat was long since over. Although not as numerous as the Jacobite commemoratives, both glass and ceramics in memory of William III were produced throughout the period for the extreme opposition to the Stuarts and Popery.

Coronation glasses of George I, although rare, were produced in some quantity and are easily recognisable owing to the introduction of the silesian moulded stem from Germany (11). With the arrival of the Hanoverian dynasty German and Dutch craftsmen came to England in large numbers and imports of German glass, although stoutly resisted by the Glass Makers' Company, reached a peak in 1714. In an attempt to stem the tide of newly fashionable imported glass the English makers copied the German style and introduced the silesian stem with the moulded inscription around the four-sided knop, *God Save King George*. The style, being fashionable, was also short-lived and had virtually vanished from English glass by 1720.

Despite the growth of the English glass industry throughout the eighteenth century and the export of English lead crystal for engraving abroad, very few Georgian Coronation glasses exist, those for George II being particularly rare (12). Two widely differing factors may have a bearing on this scarcity one being the emphasis on stem decoration which developed after 1750 and the other the disappearance of political significance in toasting the monarch. By 1735 when Benjamin Payne of the Glass Sellers' Arms in Fleet Street advertised 'the arms of all the Royal Family finely engraved on glasses' such Royal symbols have become purely decorative.

The growth of wheel engraving and cutting did not preclude other decorative techniques. Although enamelled glass had been produced in Germany and Italy from the early sixteenth century the technique did not arrive in England until 1696 and achieved importance almost a century later in the work of William and Mary Beilby who between circa 1762 and 1778 decorated Newcastle glass with enamelled designs ranging from simple vine leaves to elaborate commissioned heraldic subjects, one of the earliest and finest being that painted to commemorate the birth of the Prince of Wales in 1762. James Heming, whose friend Mrs Dixon was so fortunate in the matter of the medal, also recorded the luck of 'our friend Harry who, at the Coronation of George III, was upon the scaffold at the return of the procession, closed in with the rear; at the expense of half a guinea was admitted into the Hall; got brimful of His Majesty's claret; and in the universal plunder brought off the glass Her Majesty drank in, which is placed in the beaufet as a valuable curiosity.'[19]

Slipware and delft continued throughout the reigns of the first three Georges. A George I charger by Ralph Simpson is in the Victoria and Albert (28) and a very rare George II charger by Samuel Malkin is in the Burnap Collection, Nelson Atkins Art Gallery, Kansas. George I and III are represented frequently but crudely on delftware but again George II portrait plates are rare and the majority of dated examples seem to have been produced following the Jacobite uprisings of 1715 and 1745. Stoneware continues to use Royal symbols decoratively, and, one feels, in the case of a goblet with relief decorations of a hunt, cupid riding a lion, and busts of George III, Queen Charlotte, and George and Martha Washington, somewhat tactlessly.[20]

The greatest advances in ceramics occur in the 1750's; the dual developments of porcelain production and transfer printing revolutionised the industry and happily coincided with developments in transport and industrialisation to greatly increase the market.

The fashion for china introduced by Queen Mary had lead initially to the import of Chinese and Japanese porcelain by the rich, these Eastern imports were followed in the eighteenth century by continental imports from Germany and France. A ready market existed for a British porcelain industry and between the years 1744 and George III's Coronation in 1761 the great porcelain boom took place. Of the seven major firms founded in that period, Bow, Chelsea, Longton Hall, Worcester, Liverpool, Derby and Lowestoft, five had virtually ceased production by 1800. Transfer printing was the invention of John Brooks, an Irish engraver, who made an unsuccessful attempt to patent 'a method for printing, impressing and reversing upon enamel and china from engraved etched and mezzotint plates' in 1751.[21] By 1754 he was in partnership with Stephen Janssen and Henry Delamain in the production of enamels at York House, Battersea. These short lived enamel works were the birthplace of English transfer printing and produced the greatest exponents of the art, Simon

Francois Ravenet and his pupil Robert Hancock. From Battersea the process spread first to Bow and shortly afterwards to Worcester, Caughley and Derby. For an appreciation of the importance of transfer printing we have to turn to the oft quoted remark of John Sadler of Liverpool that 'two men transfer printing can equal the output of one hundred decorators,'[22] furthermore, transfer printing meant that the producers of commemorative pottery no longer had to rely on the artistic skill of individual decorators but could copy engravings of the finest likenesses of their subjects.

The manufacturers of enamel and porcelain soon utilised the new technique to produce portrait commemoratives. The Battersea factory issued portrait plaques of the Duke of Cumberland, Frederick Prince of Wales, Henry Pelham, George II and Lord Blakeney, Birmingham produced plaques of Elizabeth and Maria Gunning, two famous beauties of the day. The introduction of statesmen, military heroes, beauties and actresses was a new and important departure in commemorative and portrait ceramics. Prior to the 1780's portrait or commemorative items are almost entirely restricted to monarchs, as the King was essentially the only nationally famous individual whose portrait was recognisable from the coinage and whose significance was obvious. Prints of the beautiful and the heroic had been produced from the time of Elizabeth but the market for them had been the intelligentsia, who were, by definition, also the wealthy. Between 1700 and 1760 over 130 country newspapers had become established and thus knowledge of and admiration for an increasing number of national and international figures had grown to such a degree that the demand for commemorative items of the famous now exceeded the demand for commemorative items of Royalty. The most famous productions of the Chelsea factory are not figures of Royalty but figures of actors and the same was to be true of Derby and Rockingham. The increase of constitutional government and the erosion of the divine trappings of the monarch must have accelerated the change. The enamels and porcelain we are discussing were intended for the wealthy but the same process was also in operation in less refined markets.

It was as a military leader that Frederick the Great was commemorated and his image on porcelain and pottery far exceeds that of George II or George III. In 1756 Britain entered an alliance against France and the Holy Roman Empire thus marking Britain's entry into the Seven Years War. In 1757 Frederick achieved a personal victory at the Battle of Rosbach and by December of that year his portrait, engraved by Robert Hancock, appeared on Worcester porcelain. The Worcester lead was soon followed by Liverpool on both porcelain and enamel. The Battersea plaque of George II adapted by Ravenet from the engraving for the contemporary coinage by John Sigismund Tanner probably owes its existence to the alliance with Frederick in 1756 and the magnificent Longton Hall figure of Britannia seated gazing at a plaque moulded in relief with a profile portrait of George II is generally accepted as commemorating the alliance. Frederick's popularity continued into the nineteenth century and as late as August 24th 1793, Parson Woodforde purchased two figures in 'Plaister of Paris, one of the King of Prussia and another of the present Duke of York, both on horseback and coloured.'[23]

Although Royalty was fighting a losing battle with military and dramatic heroes all the world loved a wedding and that of George III and Charlotte of Mecklenburg-Strelitz in 1761 was no exception. The dates of George's marriage and Coronation are so close that some commemoratives may well be seen as either wedding or Coronation souvenirs. Images of George and Charlotte either together or singly are to be found on enamels and porcelain from the Worcester, Bow (37), Liverpool, Longton Hall, and Derby factories. Considerable care has to be taken over assigning dates to portrait commemoratives of the Royal couple. Although the engraved plates produced by both Hancock and Sadler date from 1761 they were frequently re-used throughout the reign. A Derby mug transfer printed with King George III by Richard Holdship (39) probably dates from 1764 to 1769 when Holdship was at the factory, a pair of Sadler printed Worcester tankards in the Victoria and Albert Museum date from circa 1765 (38) and the Hancock prints of the King and Queen used in Worcester in 1761 (35) were re-issued to commemorate the Jubilee.

The great advances in the pottery industry which occurred in the 1760's were too late to affect the commemorative items associated with George III's Coronation although increasing sophistication in Staffordshire earthenware resulted in some fine pieces with relief portraits of the King and Queen and one quite spectacular enamel decorated creamware teapot now in Stoke-on-Trent Museum (34). Creamware was to be further developed during the 1760's by Josiah Wedgwood and its relative cheapness was a contributory factor in the demise of many of the porcelain factories. Wedgwood began production of his portrait medallions in 1773 and produced eleven of George III including two celebrating the King's recovery from illness in 1788. Six medallions of George IV were produced, all before his accession and four of William IV as Duke of Clarence. The only Wedgwood portrait medallion which can be remotely considered a Coronation commemorative is that of Victoria.

The great advances in pottery and porcelain achieved their full potential with the growth of a literate population, increasing demand and massive improvements in communications. Although pedlars and street traders still travelled the country holding sales in inns and halls or setting up their stalls in market places the retailing of fine pieces was conducted through established warehouses and shops. Worcester estab-lished a London warehouse in 1756 and almost ten years before Horace Walpole had purchased the lease of Strawberry Hill from Mrs Chenevix a dealer in 'toys' at Charing Cross. 'It is a little plaything house that I got out of Mrs Chenevix's shop and is the prettiest bauble you ever saw',[24] he wrote to Conway on June 8th 1747. By 1775 fashionable shops were selling both porcelain and glass in London, Worcester, Bristol and Bath, and such emporia as Jerome Johnson's 'Entire Glass Shop' in the Strand could offer a wide range of fashionable items.

Improvements to the roads were carried out by the Turnpike Trusts and the great boom in road construction dates from 1788–95. James Brindley's Bridgewater Canal of 1761, although pre-dated by Henry Berry's Mersey-St. Helen's Canal of 1757, is generally seen as promoting a massive programme of canal building and its consequences were ap-preciated by Adam Smith who reported that; 'Six or eight men by the help of the water carriage, can carry and bring back in the same time the same quantity of goods between London and Edinburgh as fifty broad wheeled wagons attended by a hundred men and drawn by four hundred horses.'[25]

We can forgive his exaggeration for the late eighteenth century is an age of startling statistics provided by the industrial revolution and growing markets at home and abroad. The change in society from rural to industrial, from the small community to the large city was to be re-flected in nineteenth century Coronation commemoratives but the most significant pointer to nineteenth century developments in souvenirs is a small earthenware plate of the 1790's decorated with a design of George III presenting a Bible to a child and inscribed, 'I hope the time will come when every poor child in my dominions will be able to read the Bible.'[26]

CHAPTER FOUR   The Nineteenth Century

The three nineteenth century Coronations took place within seventeen years so it is not surprising that the commemorative items associated with them share similarities of style and purpose. The three monarchs, however, could not be more different. George IV, an elderly roué, his once exquisite taste and his figure both coarsening with age, 'he looked too large for effect, indeed he was more like an elephant than a man.'[27] wrote a Westminster schoolboy at his Coronation in 1821; William IV the bluff sailor King, a reluctant monarch and Victoria the gay romantic princess. For once the cliches aptly describe the characters.

George IV's Coronation on July 19th 1821, was the most lavish ever presented. The King designed his own costume, vaguely eastern in appearance, and supervised every aspect of this spectacular production like a Regency Cecil B. de Mille. The total cost came to £243,390 6s. 2d. which included gold and enamelled snuff boxes from Rundell and Bridge for the Foreign Ambassadors which cost over £8,000. George was the last monarch to distribute gifts of plate to the hereditary Coronation officers. Among those who traditionally received such presents were the Lord High Almoner, the Duke of Norfolk (as the Earl of Arundel, Chief Butler of England), the Lord Mayor of London, the Champion, the Cupbearer and the Barons of the Cinque Ports. The staves of the latter were frequently melted down and converted to more useful purpose, examples include a tankard, 'made of ye silver of ye Canopie when King Charles ye 2nd was crowned,' in the collection of the Goldsmiths' Company and a punch-bowl presented to the town of Hastings by the Barons after George II's Coronation. Bells which hung from the staves at the Coronations of George I, III, and IV are in the Victoria and Albert Museum collection.[28]

Commemorative items for George IV's Coronation are fewer than those recording his struggle to divorce Queen Caroline. George's own unpopularity may help to explain the almost fanatical support offered by all sections of society to this promiscuous and unattractive woman. Pro-Caroline medals have already been discussed but she was equally well supported by relatively ephemeral broadsheets and prints and by more substantial pottery commemoratives. The Willett Collection in Brighton Art Gallery contains a number of examples including a plate with a coloured portrait of 'M. Wood Esq., M.P., twice Lord Mayor of London, who patriotically gave up his House to Her Majesty Queen Caroline upon her arrival in London on the 6th June, 1820.'

The almost total absence of porcelain and glass Caroline commemoratives is largely repeated in the case of nineteenth century Coronation souvenirs. A new apolitical souvenir market had appeared largely made up of the lower middle classes and children. The commemorative was on the point of becoming the souvenir.

Linda Hannas has written, 'Until the middle of the eighteenth century there was no child in England above the age of seven,'[29] and on examination this apparently provocative statement proves to be both shrewd and true. The children of the poor, if they survived beyond the age of five, were sent to work, and the children of the rich were treated essentially as miniature adults. The beginning of the nineteenth century saw a romantic interest in children which developed into a reasonable understanding before declining under the onslaught of sentimentality and morality after 1850. The simple acknowledgement of children was not in itself sufficient to change the meaning and intention of Coronation commemoratives but in the first four decades of the nineteenth century it was combined with an equally important factor—the growth of a corporate society. The eighteenth century borough or village was run by vested interests, the Squire, the Vicar, the Magistrate and the Constable. The hierarchy was virtually self-perpetuating and small townships acted totally independently of each other. The great increase of local and national democracy came about in the 1830's. The Poor Law Amendment Act of 1834 was put into practice by locally elected trustees under the authority of a National Commission thus combining local and national resources in dealing with a social problem hitherto the sole concern of a particular town or parish. The Municipal Reform Act of 1835 instituted locally elected Borough Councils as the regular form of municipal authority and although the franchise was quite severely limited the new regime was far more democratic than the old system. Police forces sprang up throughout the 1830's and 40's thus accepting crime as a social problem requiring a social remedy. Relatively little occurred in the field of juvenile education, bedevilled as it was by religious differences, but the year 1833 saw the first annual grant of public money, £20,000 to assist the religious and charitable bodies that provided elementary schooling and an inspectorate was established to report on state aided schools. A completely new system of local democracy, corporate identity and social responsibility had been born which was to play an important role in the subsequent development of the Coronation souvenir.

When George IV was crowned in 1821 none of these reforms had been carried out but the spirit of reform was in the air and it was not surprising that his was the first Coronation to see municipal gifts to children. Manchester and Salford issued 25,697 medals to children and the Leeds Parish Church School Dinner of 1821 was eaten from excellently designed Coronation plates made in Leeds creamware (46).

The great majority of pottery made for George's Coronation was naive in character and quite possibly intended for children. Brightly coloured Prattware plates with moulded reliefs and simply transferred images are the rule and porcelain items virtually non-existent.

The increasing excellence of creamware has been mentioned as one reason for the demise of porcelain but this cannot be the sole reason and the facts point to the almost complete absence of a sophisticated or fashionable market for the nineteenth century Coronation souvenirs. The Worcester mug in the buffet had been replaced by the Staffordshire ornament on the chimney piece.

William IV's Coronation on September 8th 1831 was a mean affair. He approached the ceremony with petulance and aversion and was only forced to submit to it with difficulty. He abandoned much of the pomp and ostentation such as the procession to Westminster and the Royal Banquet, substituting a firework display for the people. He particularly objected to the exchange of kisses with the Bishops and Macaulay observed, 'The King behaved very awkwardly, his bearing making the foolish parts of the ritual appear monstrously ridiculous.'

Partly because of his dislike of ostentation William IV was exceptionally popular with the people. He was also associated with the Reform Bill which was to be passed by Parliament in 1832. The Bill sponsored by the Whig leaders Lord John Russell and Earl Grey was by no means as radical as many of its supporters would have wished but nonetheless removed the worst excesses of the electoral system. The electorate itself rose by slightly less than 50% but fifty-six rotten boroughs were dissolved and newly created seats were distributed among the rapidly growing industrial towns of the North and Midlands. The Bill was carried in Parliament partly because of the threat that the King would swamp the House of Lords with newly created Whig Peers if the Bill was rejected.

Reform pottery usually takes the form of stoneware spirit flasks but is also found in mugs. The flasks, produced in Lambeth, Chesterfield and Nottingham have shoulders and spouts modelled as the heads of the principal reformers particularly· Russell, Grey, Brougham, and the King. Several are very definitely Coronation commemoratives bearing the Coronation date together with the slogans of reform. The reverse process can be seen in examples of Coronation mugs with additional reform attributes and William's joint role as monarch and reformer is celebrated on a rare Sunderland lustre plaque with the inscription *William the IV the only Royal Reformer since Alfred.*

The metamorphosis of spirit flask into Coronation commemorative was completed in 1838 when several stoneware firms issued flasks modelled as figures of the young Queen Victoria (64) – a circumstance which she would no doubt have found unamusing in her old age. Joseph Bourne of Denby must have been among the first to produce a model as his flask bears the inscription *Queen Alexandrina Victoria* on the supposition that she would be known by her first christian name. Victorian flasks were also issued by Oldfield of Chesterfield, Green of Lambeth and Doulton, who also produced a brown saltglazed Coronation mug with relief decoration of the Royal Arms and Victoria's head in profile to the left, a pattern which influenced the same firm's Elizabeth II mug designed by Agnette Hay.

William and Adelaide were the first British monarchs to be widely commemorated by busts, a fashion that was to grow with the development of biscuit china and Parian ware in imitation of white marble which put such hitherto expensive items within the reach of the middle classes. Minton produced bisque busts of the Royal couple and white porcelainous busts were produced in Staffordshire as were full length figures in white earthenware (51), forerunners of the flatback Staffordshire figures. Minton also issued a very fine stoneware jug with moulded relief portraits of the King and Queen.[30]

The introduction in George's reign of commemorative items designed for children was continued in commemoratives of William and Victoria. A particularly charming series of transfer prints of William's Coronation is found on many items, particularly on small plates with moulded borders of flowers produced in Staffordshire and Victoria is represented by similarly moulded transferred pieces (42). A large number of utilitarian wares, particularly jugs, bear fine large transfers, often in puce, of the King and Queen and these would seem to constitute the majority of 'adult' souvenirs (49). Mugs, though few jugs, in a similar style were issued for Victoria.

If the William and Adelaide white earthenware figures can be seen as the precursors of the flatback, the only Staffordshire portrait figure definitely commemorating Victoria's Coronation must be seen as among the very first of its type. 'Her Majesty Queen Victoria' in the style of Obadiah Sherratt, is a modified version of the figure of the opera singer Maria Malibran who died on September 23rd 1836 (63). As the demand for Malibrans ceased so the demand for Victorias grew and this clever adaptation must have bridged the gap until standing figures of the Queen were produced in the 1840's. In fact the extreme rarity of this figure suggests that few were produced. Coincidentally the sculptor Charles Rivers showed a bust of Madame Malibran at the Royal Academy in 1837 and one of Victoria in 1838.

Souvenir games and dolls are first found for the Coronation of William. The jigsaw puzzle, invented by John Spilsbury in 1762 makes its debut as a Coronation memento, one being known for William's and two for Victoria's (56). The advent of the cheap colour print at the beginning of the nineteenth century no doubt encouraged the growth of the jigsaw industry and was available in the form of panoramas by Victoria's Coronation. Velvet and tinsel portraits of William and Adelaide were produced by M. and M. Skelt of the Minories., and the growth in cheap mass-produced souvenirs for children was phenomenal. Portrait dolls had become fashionable in the eighteenth century. The wealthy commissioned artists in wax to reproduce the features of their family in miniature. Probably the most famous exponent of the art was Marie Grosholtz who began her career making portrait dolls of the family of Louis XVI and ended it in England as the justly renowned Madame Tussaud. Obviously such dolls were not playthings but the moulded composition doll of Queen Adelaide must have been produced in large numbers as must the china portrait doll of Queen Victoria produced on her accession. The wax dolls of Queen Victoria in her Coronation robes would be considerably more expensive and destined for the cabinet rather than the toy cupboard (54). Dolls were later produced for Queen Alexandra, Queen Elizabeth and Queen Elizabeth II the latter being represented by a range of dolls including cheap pink moulded plastic ones dressed in tinsel to a limited edition portrait doll sanctioned by the Lord Chamberlain's Office.

Dolls were a feminine prerogative, snuff boxes a masculine one. Both George IV and William IV are represented on papier mâché snuff boxes probably produced throughout their reigns and bearing coloured transfer prints. (53) Although beauties including Jenny Lind appear on nineteenth century snuff boxes the makers tactfully refrained from using the Queen's image.

The Queen does appear on one pot-lid; 'Queen Victoria with Coronation regalia' was produced by T., J., and J. Mayer of Dale Hall Pottery, Burslem in or around 1849. Although not strictly a Coronation commemorative it is the only pot-lid to portray a monarch in Coronation robes. A similar unique commemorative item is the one Baxter Coronation print. *Her Most Gracious Majesty Queen Victoria receiving the Sacrament at her Coronation*, includes about two hundred individual portraits and finally appeared on October 1st 1841, when interest had largely subsided. The print was a financial failure partly because of the delay in publication and partly because of the high prices such a complex production necessitated, the large size $21\frac{3}{4}'' \times 17\frac{1}{2}''$ sold for 5 guineas and the small, $17\frac{1}{2}'' \times 13\frac{3}{8}''$ for 3 guineas.

Printed fabrics also appear for the first time in the nineteenth century. A number of silk and petersham ribbons have survived from George IV's Coronation and bear transferred hand coloured designs of the emblems of Royalty and loyalty (128). Victoria's celebrations produced a handkerchief printed in purple and red with the interior of Westminster Abbey decked for the Coronation. This would appear to be the progenitor of the thousands of printed handkerchiefs and scarves which have been wildly waved at subsequent Coronations. The same design is reproduced in a repeating architectural frame as a furnishing fabric. Large Coronation paper hangings and wallpapers first appear in 1902.

Commemorative glasses are fairly scarce for all three Coronations and in the case of George IV are outnumbered by glasses bearing pro-Caroline sentiments. Apsley Pellatt's invention of cameo-glass, patented as crystallo-ceramie in 1819, proved a successful if expensive medium for commemoratives. The process of embedding cameo portraits in glass proved difficult and breakages were frequent but the finished productions were of very high quality and virtually the only Coronation items designed for the luxury market. Busts of George IV, William IV and Victoria are all to be found in Pellatt paperweights (67).

Surprisingly the introduction of press-moulded glass which arrived from America c.1830 did not produce cheap glass souvenirs in 1831 but was to be put to good effect during Victoria's reign.

CHAPTER FIVE The Twentieth Century

Edward VII was crowned on August 9th 1902. Sixty-four years had passed since Victoria's Coronation and the social and industrial changes which began in the early nineteenth century had accelerated during her reign. The Great Exhibition of 1851 witnessed the skill and ingenuity of British manufacturers and craftsmen and what we now feel the Victorians to have lacked in taste they made up for in vigour and energy. The change from an agrarian to an industrial society was complete and the industrious artisan, although not wealthy, was now allowed a certain amount of leisure and could at last afford, if not the finer things in life, the fripperies. Later Victorian and Edwardian taste seemed, despite the distinctly separate efforts of Morris and Whistler, to involve the amassing of smaller objects on larger ones. Mantlepieces, tables, cabinets and delft shelves groaned under the weight of accumulated ornaments. In pursuit of this universal aim the poorer classes were well catered for by the recent souvenir industry. The Bank Holiday Act of 1871 made a day by the seaside possible for the working classes and mementoes of their annual day at Southport, Blackpool, or Scarborough were produced in vast quantities by British, German and Czechoslovakian companies. Inland towns were not ignored, the indefatigable W. H. Goss recorded almost all known historical objects and regional peculiarities on his miniature crested china, including the Coronation chair (121). Imitators abounded. Fairings, cheap pottery groups often with slightly risque subjects could be obtained as their name implies at fairs and free collectable items for the slightly wealthier were supplied by the manufacturers of pot lids. As each cheap curio, souvenir or free gift became economically impossible it was replaced by something cheaper; Goss and imitation wares, restricted to one locality by subjects and Coat of Arms, were replaced by more general multi-resort souvenirs; the spirit of the fairing by the vulgar postcard; the pot lid by the decorated tin and later by the plastic gift or illustrated card. An industry had been born and the Jubilee of Queen Victoria in 1887 had provided that industry with a dress rehearsal for King Edward's Coronation.

In June 1902 the King became ill with appendicitis, then a serious illness. The Coronation was postponed from June 26th to August 9th during which time the people prayed for his health. His recovery lead to national rejoicing and increased the Coronation fever that the rest of the nation was suffering. Edward shared certain characteristics with his forbear George IV particularly in his taste for extra marital affairs but ironically in the far staider England of 1902 this increased his popularity and the King's 'Loose Box,' a stall in the Abbey reserved for his mistresses, was the subject of jokes rather than scandal.[31]

The King's Dinner was given to the poor of London and the charitable nature of gifts for both Edward VII's and George V's Coronation is borne out in the provinces. In 1902 Liverpool gave a 'treat to the aged' and a garden party for 'working men and their wives' and of the 130,000 children who received medallions the 5,000 poorest were also given bags of food. At Aston near Birmingham hot dinners were provided for the old, poor and infirm. George V's celebrations in 1911 saw a treat to 1,300 crippled children and 450 feeble-minded children in Liverpool and whereas the elementary schoolchildren received four new halfpennies (544,000 coins) 500 crippled and invalided children were given Coronation mugs in presentation cases. In Birmingham 4,000 old people received souvenir portraits of the King and Queen and a 2s. 5d. food ticket; military veterans had the additional treat of a day in the country.

The charitable nature of the gifts, the differential between the healthy middle class and the infirm poor was further marked in some towns where the cost of gifts and celebrations was borne by the wealthy section of society. The Wolverhampton Council Minutes of March 6th 1911 recommend that the expenses of the Coronation celebrations for George V should be borne by the Council and 'not as heretofore by a few generous private individuals.' The Coronation celebrations of George VI and Elizabeth II saw a decline in this means-test distribution of gifts.

Local Government expenditure on Coronation celebrations was sanctioned by the Local Government Board. Not unnaturally expenditure increased, the Liverpool halfpennies of 1911 cost £1,133 6s. 8d., the 142,084 mugs they distributed in 1953 cost them over £11,000 and the Birmingham celebrations of 1953 cost £56,570. Wherever possible local expenditure went to local firms. Stoke's Edward VII mug was produced by George Jones and Sons Limited of Stoke, Newcastle's George V beaker by C. T. Maling and Sons Limited of Newcastle, Sheffield gave penknives, Leeds distributed mugs made by J. H. Awmack of Leeds, Liverpool gave mugs made in Liverpool. Birmingham's distribution of a Coronation mug for Edward VIII sparked off immediate local opposition. Mr. H. O. Worrall, a manufacturer of fancy leather goods, as reported in the Birmingham Gazette of 13th January 1937, suggested a leather purse with a slogan encouraging thrift as being more suitable and when the mugs were finally distributed for the Coronation not of Edward but of George VI, attention was drawn to the fact that they had been purchased through 'a Birmingham factor.' In 1953, possibly to avoid recurrence of the 1937 controversy, Birmingham offered what must have been one of the widest choices of souvenirs for children including the Bible, The New Testament, *Elizabeth Our Queen* by Richard Dimbleby, a spoon, a tankard, two varieties of mug, tins of chocolate, propelling pencils, a penknife and a portrait dish. Although the children themselves were to decide, parental and scholastic influence can be detected in the newspaper report which claimed that a resounding majority had chosen the Bible. Commercial firms were equally generous in providing Coronation gifts.

Many manufacturers had discovered that the production of cheap souvenirs combining appropriate loyal sentiments with hard sell advertising provided a large public with details of their goods and services. Others achieved wide sales for their products with distinctive Coronation containers. The introduction of stamped, pressed and transferred tin containers in the late nineteenth century revolutionised the confectionery industry by providing a longer life and a cheaper more attractive packaging for their goods. Rowntree's and Cadbury's were quick to realise the potential of Coronation commemorative boxes produced by the Metal Box Company and were later followed by Oxo and biscuit manufacturers (107). Breweries provided Coronation strong ale in specially labelled bottles to customers and employees, a practice which has continued and, with the production of a special Coronation sherry in 1953 by Harveys of Bristol, expanded into a more prestigious market. Cigarette manufacturers and tea merchants provided collectable Coronation cards (124) and many commercial interests, large and small, gave Coronation gifts to retailers, customers and staff. Wherever possible advertising incorporated Coronation motifs, overcoming enormous difficulties in doing so. The Bile Beans booklet *Curious Facts about the Coronation,* published in 1902, is actually full of curious facts about Bile Beans including 'Interesting Welsh Case – Skin Eruptions and Liver Disorder Cured,' and 'For Female Mill Workers Bile Beans are a Perfect Boon.' The Co-operative Society in an advertisement of 1911 adopts the straightforward if incongruous motto, 'Celebrate the Coronation by Joining the Co-operative Movement' (126).

The cheapness, shoddiness and charitable connections of the twentieth century Coronation souvenirs must have played a part in the emergence of the limited edition luxury commemorative that first appears in 1902. The limited edition is a twentieth century phenomenon, earlier Coronation commemoratives had been necessarily limited through smaller markets and the lack of industrial production techniques. Coupled with an awareness that the mass produced souvenir would never have the degree of rarity and therefore value of past commemorative wares was the economic fact that hand produced items would necessarily be so expensive as to eliminate all but the smallest market. The imaginative rich could still commission pieces. William Moorcroft, appointed Potter to Queen Mary in 1928, designed Coronation mugs for distribution by Lasenby Liberty to commemorate the Coronation of Edward VII and George V and a separate George V mug in an edition of 500 for Lord Norton. Those equally rich but lacking initiative or generosity were well catered for by the major producers and the high class retailers Thomas Goode of South Audley Street who commissioned limited editions from the earliest years of the century and W. H. Plummer and Company of New York who ordered a Minton bone china box in an edition of 500 for the Coronation of Edward VII. By 1953 all the major producers of porcelain, pottery and glass were issuing limited editions. Silver and jewellery manufacturers also issued limited editions delaying the stamping of their productions until the Coronation hallmark of 1953 was authorised for use (114). In Birmingham alone it was anticipated that 2,000 articles a day would be stamped. The relative austerity of post-war Britain produced a situation in which the market for luxury goods could not be satisfied and wherever possible manufacturers seized the opportunity that the Coronation year relaxation of laws and taxes afforded them. There was even a limited edition handmade Queen Elizabeth Doll 'as approved by the Coronation authorities.'

The Birmingham Mail of November 17th 1936 recorded the rejoicing in Birmingham at the announcement of a hundred per cent import duty on imported Coronation souvenirs while regretting that 'the belated decision has allowed Japanese, German and Czecho-Slovakian goods to enter the market somewhat freely.' In 1953 foreign souvenir imports were banned and the purchase tax lifted on souvenirs.

Full lead crystal, for long denied to the British public, was made available for the first time since the war. Not unnaturally many foreign goods did manage to reach retail outlets and their shoddiness was a cause for concern to the British manufacturers who were prevented from vulgar excesses by the Lord Chamberlain's control over the use of the Royal Cypher and Coat of Arms and the recommendations of their own professional bodies. The Federation of British Pottery manufacturers produced an official design for members for both the 1937 and 1953 Coronations (95) and in 1937 the Federation of British Industry set up a Coronation Medal Committee to approve British designs. The relatively unexciting nature of recent Coronation commemoratives must be a result of these arbiters of good taste. Some few manufacturers did attempt to give their products a more contemporary look by employing artists as designers. Wedgwood, a company with a great tradition of artist designers produced a 1937 mug designed by Eric Ravilious for the Coronation of Edward VIII (89) and a 1953 mug by Richard Guyatt (92). Dame Laura Knight produced a design for Edward VIII's Coronation used by Johnson Brothers (85) and Bernard Leach made stoneware mugs for Elizabeth II's Coronation (93). Overall however, twentieth century commemoratives are tastefully undistinguished and in 1953 both Doulton and Royal Worcester produced items reflecting the past rather than the present, the former echoing that factory's Victoria Coronation mug and the latter a bell-shaped tankard of the Dr. Wall period.

The commercial aspects of the twentieth century Coronation commemorative are nowhere better illustrated than during the brief reign and abdication of Edward VIII. From October 1936 and Mrs Simpson's divorce in Ipswich (headlined in an American paper as 'King's Moll Reno'd in Wolsey's Home Town') until the actual announcement on December 11th, speculation over the Abdication was rife and the manufacturers who had already started production of souvenirs understandably worried. The Birmingham Despatch's headline of the 4th December 1936 reads, 'Birmingham Coronation Orders Are Being Cancelled—Huge Trade Loss if the King Abdicates.' The King did abdicate but the 'Huge Trade Loss' did not occur. Not only did the Coronation of the new King which still took place on the 18th May provide further orders but those souvenirs already produced found a ready market.

Various Government attempts were made to prevent the retailing of wares commemorating Edward, tin boxes were to be defaced, manufacturers were to release no further assignments, mugs were to be rendered useless. Public sympathy for Edward was not influenced by Governmental edicts, commercial considerations outweighed those of propriety and a large number of souvenirs and commemoratives found their way onto the market. Several firms adapted existing designs to provide George's souvenirs, others incorporated both monarchs. Royal Brierley Crystal seized the opportunity of commemorating the year of the three Kings with their Three Kings Decanter, to be followed in 1953 with the 'Three Queens.' What could have been a financial disaster proved to be the opposite.

The twentieth century Coronations produced a widening gap between the commemorative and the souvenir, the limited and expensive, and the available and cheap. In the former investment replaced loyalty, the latter available to all, lost even its charitable significance. Perhaps in the future the vastly expensive Coronation celebrations will assume a more useful pattern. The practice of planting Coronation trees was widely adopted in 1937 and 1953 on both a modest civic scale and in the two great Coronation plantations incorporating the Royal Cyphers of George and Elizabeth at Mynydd Du and Knighton respectively. Our growing ecological and conservationist awareness may result in more useful civic celebrations at future Coronations but the Coronation mug, with its grand antecedents in the reigns of Charles II and George III will no doubt remain the most fitting memento of Coronations past and to come.

References

1. Robert Southey. *Letters from England*. 1807. Letter XXI.
2. *Diary and Correspondence of John Evelyn*, edited by William Barry, 1854. Vol. III.pp. 294–302.
3. Ibid. Vol. I. May 29th 1660. p.337.
4. The Diary of Samuel Pepys. Tuesday April 23rd 1661.
5. James Heming. Letter in Annual Register 1761.
6. In a Council minute of 28th July 1911, the Mayor of Wolverhampton records the receipt of his Coronation medal.
7. The first Coronation stamps were those produced by Newfoundland for the Coronation of King George V. All subsequent Coronations have been commemorated.
8. A commemorative crown was also struck for the Coronation of George VI as were commemorative sovereigns with plain edges which, unlike the crowns, were not legal tender.
9. Evelyn, op.cit. Vol I. p.251.
10. Ibid. Vol. I. p.330.
11. *The Coronation of His Most Gracious Majestie King Charles the Second at Manchester. By William Heawood, Gentleman.* Edited by W. H. Ford. 1861. Manchester Local History Reference Library.
12. Constable's Accounts 1700–1750. Wolverhampton Public Libraries.
13. Quoted by W. A. Thorpe. *English Glass*, A. & C. Black, 1961.
14. Ibid.
15. Paper to the English Ceramic Circle, 1934.
16. Daniel Defoe, *A Tour Through the Whole Island of Great Britain*, 1724.
17. Sold at Sotheby's. 29th July 1971.
18. *The Selected Letters of Lady Mary Wortley-Montagu*, edited by Robert Helsbord. Longmans, 1970, p.64.
19. Heming. op.cit.
20. Sold Sotheby's, May 26th 1970.
21. Quoted by M. S. Morris, *English Enamels*, Wolverhampton Art Gallery, 1973.
22. Ibid.
23. Woodeforde's Diary. August 24th, 1973.
24. Quoted in *Horace Walpole* by R. W. Ketton-Cremer. University Paperbacks, 1964, p.12.
25. Quoted in *The First Industrial Nation* by Peter Mathias. Methuen, 1969, p.108.
26. Willett Collection, Brighton Museum and Art Gallery.
27. Quoted by Lawrence Tanner in *The History of the Coronation*. New York, 1953.
28. See *Gift Plate from Westminster Hall Coronation Banquets* by Edward Perry. Apollo Coronation Number. June, 1953.
29. Linda Hannas, *The English Jigsaw Puzzle 1760–1890*, Waylands, 1972.
30. Illustrated in Geoffrey Godden, *Illustrated Encyolopaedia of British Pottery and Porcelain*, Barrie and Jenkins, 1966, p.234.
31. See Philip Magnus, *King Edward VII*, Penguin, 1967, p.370.
32. Rupert Gunnis, *A Dictionary of British Sculpture 1660–1851*, Abbey Library, 1968.

1. The gold Coronation medal of Edward VI by Henry Basse. $2\frac{5}{16}''$ diam. Electrotype. *Wolverhampton Art Gallery and Museums*

2. The gold Coronation medal of Charles II by Thomas Simon. 1$\frac{3}{16}$" diam. Electrotype. *Wolverhampton Art Gallery and Museums*

3. The gold Coronation medal of George I by Ehrenreich Hannibal. 2" diam. Electrotype. *Wolverhampton Art Gallery and Museums*

4. The silver Coronation medal of George III by John Kirk. 1⅝″ diam. Electrotype. *Wolverhampton Art Gallery and Museums*

5. Edward VII Coronation medal in bronzed alloy issued by the Wolverhampton Union. The obverse die of the King was particularly popular with local Coronation Committees. 1¾″ diam. *Wolverhampton Art Gallery and Museums*

6. Edward VII bronze medal commemorating the Coronation visit of their Majesties to the City of London on October 25th, 1902. Produced by Searle and Co. This large medal is a typical example of those produced for subscribers during the heyday of English medal collecting which dated from the 1860's to 1910. 3″ diam. *Wolverhampton Art Gallery and Museums*

7. Elizabeth II Crown piece, minted as an alternative to an official Coronation medal. *Private Collection*

8. The Dier Glass. A brownish crystal glass goblet engraved with a hunt and the Royal Arms in diamond point and inscribed *John* or *Jone Dier*, 1581. From the London Glasshouse of Giacomo Verzelini, probably engraved by Anthony de Lisle. One of the earliest examples of English engraved glass. 8⅛″ h. *Victoria and Albert Museum*

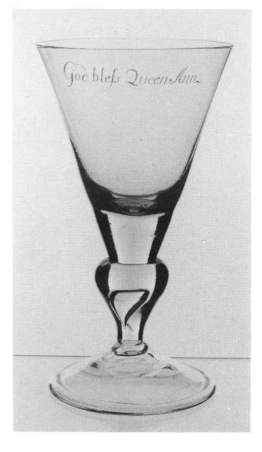

9. Dutch goblet. Crystal glass engraved in diamond point with the Royal Arms of William III and inscribed, *God Bless the King*. This glass was no doubt engraved in Holland for export to England on the accession of William and Mary to the British throne. Many commemorative medals, glasses and ceramics were produced in William's homeland to celebrate his English reign. 8⅜″ h. *Victoria and Albert Museum*

10. English goblet. Clear, colourless lead glass engraved in diamond point with the inscription, *God Bless Queen Ann*. The invention of lead glass by Ravenscroft in the late 1670's revolutionised both the making and engraving of glass. By Anne's reign the process had developed to a degree that allowed such magnificent, weighty and simple glasses as the one illustrated to be produced. 10⅝″ h. *Victoria and Albert Museum*

11. Silesian stemmed wine glass. A lead crystal glass with four-sided moulded stem bearing the inscription, *God Save King George*, one word being moulded on each side of the stem. A typical Coronation commemorative glass for George I who introduced the silesian or moulded pedestal stem from his native Hanover. Circa 1714. 6⅜″ h. *Victoria and Albert Museum*

12. German covered goblet. Lead crystal glass wheel engraved with the Royal Arms of George II, probably by G. E Kunckel of Gothe, Germany, one of the finest engravers of his time. Circa 1730. Coronation glasses of George II are extremely rare and this superb glass, formerly in the Royal Collection, was probably commissioned by George during the early years of his reign. 11″ h. *Victoria and Albert Museum*

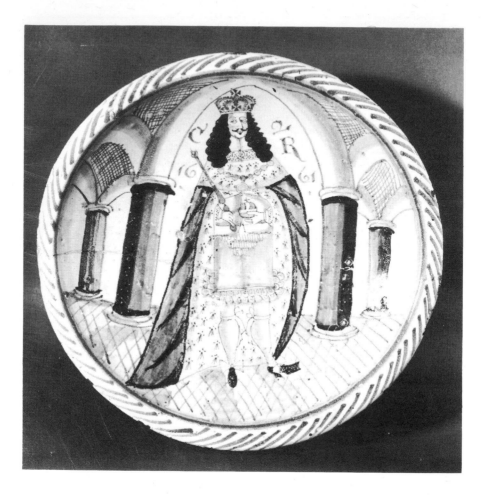

13. London delft charger. Blue dash charger with a full length portrait of Charles II in an architectural setting. Inscribed *C R 2* and dated 1661. This magnificent piece is among the earliest Charles II delft portrait plates, actually made in Coronation year. The barrel-vaulted background appears in a degenerate form on the William III charger (20). 12½″ diam. *Birmingham City Museum*

14. & 15. Two London delft wine cups. Both cups bear half length portraits of Charles II and were produced in 1660, the year of accession and 1661, Coronation year. *The London Museum*

All three pieces seem to have a common source, presumably an engraving, and show the King in the ceremonial robes in which he was painted by John Michael Wright shortly after the Coronation. The quality of the painting would suggest a fairly sophisticated and wealthy market.

16. London majolica charger. The half length portraits of Charles and Catherine of Braganza are contained within a trophy of arms and a border of fantastic animals. This very rare plate was probably produced to commemorate the marriage of Charles and Catherine in 1663. 13″ diam. *Victoria and Albert Museum*

17. Brislington delft charger, bearing a stylised portrait of Charles II inscribed *C R 2*, within a flower painted border. 12¾" diam. *Casimir Smith Collection*

These two chargers show the different influences of Holland and Italy. The latter has a blue flowered border recalling the Dutch interpretation of Chinese porcelain, the former has a typically Italian grotesque border in polychrome. The majolica piece was almost certainly commissioned and is something of an oddity among English delft portrait chargers.

A detail from the Coronation procession of King Charles II, 1661, from an etching by Wenceslas Hollar (1607–1677). *London Museum*

18. English delft bleeding bowl. Made either in Lambeth or Brislington, the bowl bears a half-length portrait of James II, inscribed *I R 2* with a laureate wreath. The handle bears the initials *P N M* and the date *1686*, the year following the Coronation. This bowl is an extremely rare example as only four dated James II pieces have been recorded. 5½″ diam. *Birmingham City Museum*

19. A pair of English delft plates, one with half-length portraits of William and Mary (8⅝″ diam.), the other with a half-length portrait of Anne with a stylised foliate border (9″ diam.). These small plates, amusingly but crudely painted, were presumably intended for a cheaper market than the large chargers. *Casimir Smith Collection*

20. Bristol delft charger showing a full length portrait of William III in armour but carrying the Coronation regalia. The arched background is a debased form of the barrel-vaulted setting of Charles II (13). Williamite portrait chargers appear both during the King's reign and throughout the first half of the eighteenth century. The example shown was probably produced during the reign but after the Battle of the Boyne, as the armour would suggest a soldier King. Later Williamite chargers usually show the King mounted. 13$\frac{1}{2}$" diam. *Victoria and Albert Museum*

21. Bristol delft plaque. A fine portrait plaque of Queen Anne after the portrait by Sir Godfrey Kneller. A similar plaque after the portrait by J.B. Closterman and attributed to Lambeth was sold at Sotheby's on June 4th 1968, for £1000. The Lambeth plaque is dated verso 1704 and the rim had been over painted in black, presumably on the Queen's death. Such plaques must have been expensive one-off items and are very rare. 9″ × 7¼″. *Victoria and Albert Museum*

22. London delft charger. This blue dash charger bears a full-length portrait of Queen Anne. A typical example with anonymous features and a stylised background, such items would have been produced throughout her reign. *London Museum*

23. This very fine Bristol delft bowl has a sophisticated floral design on the exterior and is inscribed in the well, *Long Live King George the 3d. Bristol City Museum*

24. Pair of English delft plates, (each 8⅝" diam) the one with a portrait of George I within a geometric border, the other with an unusual profile portrait of George III wearing the Garter star. *Casimir Smith Collection*

Delftware portraying the Georges makes little attempt to produce an accurate likeness. Dated pieces suggest that the majority of George I items commemorate the failure of the 1715 Jacobite Rebellion and those for George II the failure of the '45. Pieces for George III are extremely rare and mostly date from the early years of his reign.

25. Slipware charger. An earthenware dish with slip decoration showing the crowning of King Charles II by Archbishop Juxon, signed by George Taylor, and made in Burslem, Staffordshire between 1670 and 1680. A similar dish by William Taylor (17½″ diam.) is in the Manchester City Art Gallery. These Coronation dishes were produced throughout the reign. *Fitzwilliam Museum, Cambridge*

26. Slipware dish. An earthenware dish with slip decoration showing a bust portrait of Queen Anne, signed by John Wright and dated 1707. Made in Staffordshire. Another Queen Anne dish by Wright (16¾″ diam.) is in the British Museum. *Stoke on Trent Museum*

27. Slipware charger. An earthenware dish with slip decoration of the Royal Arms, attributed to Thomas Toft and made in Staffordshire circa 1680. *Stoke on Trent Museum*

28. Slipware dish. An earthenware dish with slip decoration showing a standing figure of George I and signed by Ralph Simpson. Made in Burslem circa 1715. The decorative heads in the border are a common feature of Royal slipware. The last monarch to be commemorated in slipware appears to have been George II; a dish by Samuel Malkin is in the Burnap Collection, Nelson Atkins Art Gallery, Kansas. *Victoria and Albert Museum*

29. Brown saltglaze tankard with applied Queen Anne excise stamp. Excavated from the George Hotel site in Burslem. Circa 1710. *Stoke on Trent Museum*

30. Red earthenware teapot with applied decoration of George II, Queen Caroline, crowns and foliate Tudor rose. An example from George's reign of the decorative use of Royal portraits, cyphers and emblems which developed from the excise stamps. Staffordshire, 1730–50. 6½″ h. *Willett Collection, Brighton Museum & Art Gallery*

31. Redware jug with blackglaze decoration of George II, flowers and the cypher *G R* with each letter crowned. *God Bless King George* is inscribed near the rim. It was produced in Jackfield, Shropshire probably after the '45 Jacobite Rebellion. Interestingly, a number of pro-Jacobite items were also produced at Jackfield. 6½″ h. *Willett Collection, Brighton Museum & Art Gallery*

32. Tea caddy. Staffordshire lead glazed earthenware with moulded crowned profile heads of George III and Queen Charlotte on the longer sides. Circa 1760–70. A number of polychrome caddies bearing applied relief figures of George and Charlotte are known. Despite the relatively crude and naive appearance of most of them the cost of tea implies a reasonably wealthy purchaser. $4\frac{1}{8}'' \times 4'' \times 8\frac{3}{4}''$. *Stoke on Trent Museum*

33. Bilston enamel plaque. Oval medallion painted in enamel colours on copper with a head and shoulders portrait of King George III after the engraving by William Pether from the portrait by Thomas Frye. Circa 1761. $4\frac{1}{2}'' \times 3\frac{3}{8}''$. *Wolverhampton Art Gallery and Museums*

34. Creamware teapot painted in enamel colours with a portrait of George III after the Pether engraving. Leeds or Staffordshire, circa 1765. *Stoke on Trent Museum*

The use of transfer prints on commemorative ceramics was to bring uniformity to the reproduction of engravings. The enamel plaque was probably painted over a transfer as several identical copies are known to exist; the teapot bears a fairly free interpretation of Pether's engraving. Both these items would have been produced for the luxury market.

35. Pair of first period Worcester tankards. Porcelain transfer printed in purple with portraits of Queen Charlotte and King George III. Both transfers are the work of Robert Hancock, the former probably from the engraving by Francois Aliamet in Smollett's *Continuation of the Complete History of England* (1761) and the latter from the engraving by James McArdell after the painting by Jeremiah Meyer. The engravings date from 1762 and 1761 respectively. The tankards, dating from 1762, have a dual commemorative role celebrating both the marriage and Coronation of the royal couple. Two versions of each transfer exist. The transfers were reused in 1809 to celebrate the King's Jubilee of 1810. $3\frac{1}{2}''$ h. *Casimir Smith Collection*

The tankards flank an oblong enamel box, probably a table snuff, made in Birmingham circa 1761. The box is transfer printed in pink with a similar portrait of the King after an engraving by William Woolett from the profile portrait by Alan Ramsay. The inside lid bears a portrait of Charlotte after Ramsay and the base a translation by Thomas Parnell from Pervigilium Veneris, *Let him love now/who never lov'd before/Let him who ever lov'd/now love the more.* Although often referred to as a Coronation box, the inscription would suggest a memento of marriage rather than crowning. $1\frac{5}{8}'' \times 3\frac{5}{8}'' \times 2\frac{3}{4}''$. *Wolverhampton Art Gallery & Museums*

36. First period Worcester mug printed with a Hancock transfer of Queen Charlotte but lacking the rococo scroll and with an additional inscription. Similar mugs have the King's portrait. $3\frac{5}{16}''$ h. *National Museum of Wales*

37. Bow porcelain mug transfer printed with a portrait of Queen Charlotte probably by Richard Holdship. Holdship was Hancock's employer at Worcester and appears at times to have obtained credit due to Hancock. This was probably printed in Worcester circa 1762. 5″ h. *Cheltenham Art Gallery and Museum*

38. Large tankard, first period Worcester, transfer printed with a portrait of Queen Charlotte by John Sadler of Liverpool. It is one of a pair, the other bearing the portrait of the King. Smaller identical designs were printed by Sadler on Worcester, Liverpool and Longton Hall porcelain. 6″ h. *Victoria and Albert Museum*

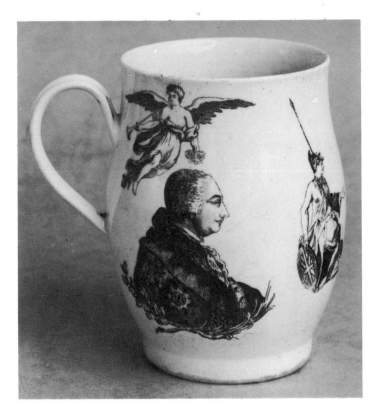

39. Derby porcelain mug transfer printed with a portrait of George III by Richard Holdship. Holdship joined the Derby factory in 1764 which means that this mug must have been either printed in Worcester or produced after Holdship's arrival. c.5″ h. *Royal Crown Derby*

The practice of supplying whiteware to printers and wholesalers in London, Liverpool and Worcester accounts for the apparent paradox of Worcester prints on Bow and Liverpool transfers on Worcester. The transfers of George and Charlotte appear throughout their reign but the orginal purpose was definitely to commemorate their wedding and Coronation.

40. Creamware plate with a basket weave border and a moulded profile portrait of George IV in the well. Inscribed, *King George IIII*. Probably Staffordshire. 8¼″ diam. *Casimir Smith Collection*

Earthenware plate with an elaborate moulded border of Royal and ecclesiastical emblems surrounding a moulded representation of the actual crowning of George IV. Inscribed, *Coronation of George IV*. 7½″ diam. *Casimir Smith Collection*

41. Earthenware mug transfer printed in black with part of the Coronation procession of William IV and, verso, a half length portrait of the King. 4½″ h. *London Museum*

42. Earthenware plate with moulded animal border surrounding a black transfer print of the Champion's challenge. Inscribed, *Coronation of King William the Fourth*. $6\frac{11}{16}''$ diam. *Casimir Smith Collection*

Earthenware mug with pie crust rim and base. Transfer printed in black with a portrait of William IV and, verso, the crowning. $4\frac{1}{2}''$ h. *Casimir Smith Collection*

43. Earthenware plate with moulded alphabet border surrounding a profile bust of Queen Victoria overglazed in polychrome. 6″ diam. *Casimir Smith Collection*

Earthenware plate with moulded floral border surrounding a puce transfer print of Queen Victoria. $6\frac{5}{8}''$ diam. *Casimir Smith Collection*

All the items shown here were probably intended for use by children.

44. White earthenware mug, transfer printed, with the inscription, *Queen Victoria, Crowned 28th June 1838, Hoghton Tower. Harris Museum and Art Gallery, Preston*

45. White earthenware mug, transfer printed with rim decoration, inscribed profile portrait of Victoria and lettered, *Success to the Town and Trade of Preston.* The form of the inscription is reminiscent of the late eighteenth and nineteenth century electioneering pottery, the forbears of local Coronation commemoratives. *Harris Museum and Art Gallery, Preston*

46. Creamware plate, transfer printed in black with an extremely elegant design of the Crown and National flowers, inscribed, *George IV crown'd July 19th 1821*. These plates were made in Leeds for the Leeds Parish Church School Dinner and are now very rare. 9″ diam. *Casimir Smith Collection*

The practice of presenting local Coronation commemoratives began in the early nineteenth century but did not become widespread until 1902. These three items must be among the earliest local souvenirs.

47. English lead crystal glass, wheel engraved with the Champion toasting the King, the Royal Cypher of George IV and the Coronation date, July 19th, 1821. George, probably inspired by the newly fashionable mediaevalism, had reintroduced full armour for the Champion and thus unwittingly emphasised the purely decorative role of that hereditary official. $5\frac{1}{4}''$ h. *Victoria and Albert Museum*

48. Earthenware mug, transfer printed in purple with a crown in a garland of national flowers and half length portraits of William and Adelaide. Inscribed, *King William IV and Queen Adelaide crowned Sep. 8 1831.* 3⅜″ h. *Private Collection*

49. Earthenware jug, transfer printed in mauve with identical transfers to the mug and additional decoration round the base and rim. 7″ h. *Laing Art Gallery, Newcastle upon Tyne*

50. & 51. Earthenware mug transfer printed in puce with the crown amid national flowers and bust portraits of the Duchess of Kent and Queen Victoria. These mugs were also produced with two identical transfers of the Queen. 4½″ h. *London Museum*

Not surprisingly, given the comparative proximity of the Coronations, these mugs closely resemble those produced for William and Adelaide.

A. The gold Coronation medal of Edward VI by Henry Basse ($2\frac{5}{16}''$ diameter)

British Museum

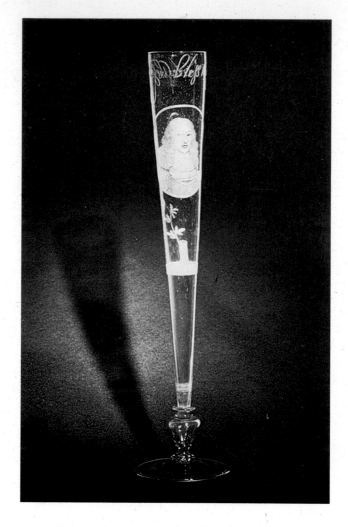

B. The Exeter Flute. English soda glass engraved in diamond point with the head of the King and inscribed, *God Bless King Charles the Second.* Probably engraved by a Dutch craftsman working in England. Once thought to be a Coronation Glass, the Exeter Flute was probably used at a banquet given for Charles by the Mayor of Dorchester in 1665, which was attended by Daniel Arden in whose family it remained until it was bequeathed to the Exeter Museum. Another possible source is a banquet given for the King by the Mayor of Exeter in 1670. Whatever its origin this glass remains one of the earliest Royal commemoratives. (17″ high)

Royal Albert Memorial Museum, Exeter

C. Slipware charger of Charles II by Ralph Simpson. 1670–80. (17¼″ diameter)

Messrs Sotheby & Co Ltd

D. London delft plate of William and Mary. Circa 1690.

Victoria and Albert Museum

E. Pair of blue dash chargers of Queen Anne and George I. (Anne 14″
   diameter; George 13¼″ diameter)

Messrs Sotheby & Co Ltd

F. Stoneware reform flask of William IV. ($7\frac{4}{5}''$ high)

Private Collection

G. A collection of Edward VIII Coronation commemorative pottery and porcelain.

Miss P. A. Burd Collection

H. Plate, cup and saucer designed and produced by Clarice Cliff for the Coronation of Elizabeth II.

Gill Jackson Collection

52. Earthenware mug transfer printed in black with two identical portraits of the seated Queen Victoria overlooking Windsor Castle. Overglazed with pink mottled lustre and probably made in Newcastle upon Tyne 4⅝″ h. *Laing Art Gallery, Newcastle upon Tyne*

The lustre of the North East provides few examples of Coronation commemoratives despite the many souvenir items these potteries produced.

53. Papier mâché snuff box with a colour transfer portrait of George IV on the lid. Inscribed, *His Most Gracious Majesty George 4th.* 3¼″ diam. *Private Collection*

Papier mâché snuff box with a painted portrait of George IV after the picture by Sir Thomas Lawrence in the Wallace Collection. 4″ diam. *Wolverhampton Art Gallery & Museum*

Papier mâché snuff box with a colour transfer print of William IV on the lid. Inscribed, *William IV King of England.* 3¼ diam. *Private Collection*

54. Wax doll of the young Queen Victoria. English circa 1838. *London Museum*

55. Queen Victoria in her Coronation robes. English, circa 1838. Head, bust and arms of wax, body of stuffed kid, wooden legs. 23½″ h. *Victoria and Albert Museum*

56. Dissected puzzle or Jigsaw puzzle of the *Coronation of William IV and Queen Adelaide*. Coloured engraving mounted on wood. Made by J. Axtell. $7\frac{1}{8}'' \times 13\frac{3}{4}''$ *Hampshire County Museum Service*

Jigsaw puzzle, *The Coronation of Queen Victoria Ist at Westminster Abbey*. Hand coloured engraving mounted on wood. The original box bears half the engraving as a label, an ingenious economic device. $7\frac{1}{2}'' \times 12''$ *Linda Hannas Collection*

Two jigsaws are recorded by Mrs Hannas for Victoria's Coronation; the other, *The Grand Coronation of Queen Victoria. June 28, 1838* measures $7'' \times 10\frac{3}{4}''$.

57. White glazed earthenware figures of Queen Adelaide and King William IV produced at the time of their Coronation. These extremely rare figures are the immediate forerunners of the more familiar Staffordshire portrait figures and flat-backs. Adelaide 13¼″ h. William 13½″ h. *Willett Collection, Brighton Museum & Art Gallery*

58. White biscuit porcelain figure of William IV on a sofa. Not a Coronation piece but an early example of parian type ware. Minton produced biscuit figures of William and Adelaide. 4½″ h. 5″ long. *Willett Collection, Brighton Museum and Art Gallery*

59. White biscuit porcelain figure of the young Queen Victoria by Minton circa 1838. 8½″ h. *Willett Collection, Brighton Museums and Art Gallery*

Parian and allied figures of Victoria were widely produced throughout her reign, particularly after the Jubilee celebrations. A Lambeth white stoneware figure is also in the Willett Collection and among later pieces there is also an elaborate Worcester parian bust of the elderly Queen on a pedestal, measuring 25″ in height. Worcester also produced parian busts of Edward VII and Alexandra. Unmarked busts of George V and Queen Mary are among the final parian productions.

60. A pair of busts of King George V and Queen Mary in bisque china. Unmarked. Each 4½″ h. *Collection Gill Jackson*

61. Fine large parian bust of Queen Mary, one of a pair. c.12″ h. *Private Collection*

The last major parian royal busts are those for King George V and Queen Mary but throughout the twentieth century small pairs of busts in a variety of media were produced for each Coronation. At the 1937 and 1953 Coronations metal busts outnumber ceramic ones although particularly unpleasant plaster and plastic portrait models of Elizabeth II are quite numerous.

62. *Left and centre* Metal busts of King George VI and Queen Elizabeth in spelter. Signed G. H. Paulin and stamped, Made in England. 4″ h. *Private Collection*
Right A moulded bisque china bust of Edward VII in the Coronation Robes with the plinth inscribed, June 26 1902. This was probably made in Germany and would be one of a pair. 4½″ h. *Private Collection*

63. Staffordshire white glazed earthenware figure in the style of Obadiah Sherratt of the seated Queen Victoria. This figure, probably produced on the Queen's accession in 1837, was adapted from the portrait figure of Maria Malibran, 1808–1836, the popular opera singer. The original figure was based on the engraving of Malibran by J. Rogers after A. M. Huffam. Maria died on September 23rd 1836 and the figure was swiftly altered to produce a commemorative item for Victoria's accession on June 20th 1837. The extreme rarity of the figure suggests that few were actually produced. 10½" h. *Private Collection*
Photograph by Jane Gate, courtesy of John Hall and David MacWilliams Antiques

64. & 65. English stoneware flask modelled as the young Victoria. The impressed inscription verso, *Queen Alexandrina Victoria*, suggests a date between the Queen's Accession in 1837 and her Coronation in 1838. The flask bears no maker's mark. 6″ h. *Collection Roger Green*

66. Apsley Pellatt cut glass toilet water bottle with profile head of William
IV. *Cheltenham Art Gallery and Museum*

67. Clear glass paperweight enclosing an opaque ceramic paste cameo bust of Queen Victoria. Made by Apsley Pellatt, circa 1838. *Victoria and Albert Museum*

Pellatt's process of crystallo-ceramie or cameo incrustation was patented in 1819. As his own title implies he had developed his technique from that of the Frenchman Desprez, who was enclosing white porcellaneous cameos in crystal glass in the first decade of the nineteenth century. The example shown is relatively simple for a Pellatt piece.

68. Porcelain teapot with a crown-shaped lid, transfer printed over relief decoration. This teapot, like most Edwardian commemoratives, bears the wrong Coronation date. A rare example of robustness and suitability combined in a Coronation item. Printed mark of Samuel Redford Ltd. 7″ h. *Stoke on Trent Museum and Art Gallery*

69. Creamware teapot with coloured transfer print of Edward VIII and blue hand-painted decoration. Stamped on the base, Gibsons, England. 4″ h. *Author's Collection*

70. Vitreous stoneware plate, transfer printed in brown. Presented to the citizens of Worcester by the Mayor, Mr Walter Holland, as an Edward VII Coronation gift. Printed mark of Royal Worcester, England. 9¼″ diam. *Author's Collection*

Royal Worcester produced a similar plate in green as the gift of Mr Emmanuel Thomas, Mayor of Worcester, in the year of George V's Coronation.

71. & 72. Earthenware beaker transfer printed in green. Printed mark, Royal Doulton Ltd. England. Rd. No. 389307. 3¾″ h. *Author's Collection*

These beakers were presented by King Edward VII to the children of London who attended the Coronation Dinners in the London Parks. Doulton had previously produced a Jubilee beaker, designed by John Slater, in 1887. One hundred thousand Jubilee beakers were produced of which forty-five thousand were ordered by Edward, then Prince of Wales. The King ordered half a million Coronation beakers and was shown designs by Slater when he granted an audience to Mr Ronald Doulton. According to Doulton, the King said; 'I want something similar to the one you did for Queen Victoria's Jubilee', and sketched the design for the beaker himself. Doulton produced three other designs of fine earthenware beakers for the 1902 Coronation.

73. White porcelain mug decorated with a hand coloured transfer of the
Royal cypher of Edward VII. The base conceals a lithophane portrait of
the King, visible when held up to the light. Made by Minton. 2⅝″ h.
Wolverhampton Art Gallery and Museum

74. White porcelain mug decorated with a colour transfer print of the
Royal cypher of George V with a lithophane portrait of the King in the
base, The mug bears the arms of Altrincham, Cheshire on the reverse and
was presumably a Coronation gift. 2⅝″ h. *Author's Collection*

Front views of the mugs opposite, with a similar white porcelain Edward
VII cup in the centre. $2\frac{3}{4}''$ h. *Author's Collection*

Lithophane portrait mugs and cups were certainly produced of Queen
Alexandra and probably of Queen Mary. The lithophane process was
invented by Baron de Bourgoing of Paris who took out a patent in 1827.
The English licensee was Robert Griffiths Jones of London who disposed
of the manufacturing rights to Grainger Lee and Co. of Worcester.
Lithophanes were produced by Minton and Coalport after the expiry of
the patent in 1877.

75. White earthenware mug with hand-painted transfer decoration bearing the rare correct date for Edward VII's Coronation and a white earthenware colour transfer printed mug for the Coronation of George V. *London Museum*

76. Twenty-four piece tea service bearing fine colour transfer prints of George V and Queen Mary. The King is depicted in two different uniforms, a red military one and a blue naval one. Individual pieces of the set were sold separately, mugs and ashtrays being the most commonly found. Manufactured by Royal Doulton. *Private Collection*

77. *Left* Earthenware plate, transfer printed in black with a homing pigeon, recording the success of Mr Aaron Sykes' birds in the Glossop, Hadfield and District Homing Society's season of 1911. The plate bears sepia tinted portraits of George and Mary and the design suggests that this Coronation plate was specifically produced for local over-printing. 10¼″ diam. *Casimir Smith Collection*

Right Earthenware plate transfer printed in blue with an elaborate design of the King and Queen and the might of the Royal Navy. The plate is over-printed with a local inscription and the arms of *Middlesboro-on-Tees*. Presumably intended as a gift for those attending the ox-roasting, a popular form of celebration particularly in the North East. 9½″ diam. *Casimir Smith Collection*

78. Two-handled bone china loving cup, transferred and hand painted decoration on an apple green ground. Bust portraits of King George V and Queen Mary on the front and a list of the colonies in a cartouche supported by putti, verso. Inside the rim are oak leaf garlands and shields bearing the names of the Royal children including Prince John, the youngest child who died at Sandringham as a boy. The piece is marked on the base, Spode Copeland's China, England. Souvenir. Coronation George V 1911. Edition de luxe. Limited to 100 copies. T. Goode and Co. South Audley St. London W. No. 15. 7½″ h. *Commemorative Collectors' Society*

Thomas Goode were and are among the premier retailers of limited edition ceramics and glass. Goode's commissioned luxury commemorative items from the beginning of the twentieth century, a Boer War mug of 1901 and a Nelson Victory mug of 1905, both by Spode, were among the first.

79. & 80. Stoneware two-handled loving cups of Edward VIII and George VI by Royal Doulton. Doulton had previously produced a three-handled loving cup for the Coronation of George V and a two-handled cup for the 1935 Jubilee in an edition of 1000. The Edward VIII loving cup was in two sizes, the large size in an edition of 2000 and the small in an edition of 1000. The Abdication caused production to cease when 1080 large cups and 454 small cups had been made. The design was cleverly adapted with the minimum of change and cups in the same sizes and editions commemorate the Coronation of George VI and Queen Elizabeth. The large size, with a height of 10½″ sold for 55s. and the small for 30s. All the cups are numbered on the base. *Royal Doulton Ltd.*

81. & 82. Small size Edward VIII loving
cup with reverse portrait of the King as
the Prince of Wales. *Royal Doulton Ltd.*

83. & 84. Queen Elizabeth II loving cup in earthenware with under-glaze decoration (10″ h.). Only one size of this cup was made in an edition of 2000. A saltglaze stoneware loving cup with carved, incised and modelled decoration was designed for Royal Doulton by Agnette Hay in an edition of 100. *Royal Doulton Ltd.*

85. Dame Laura Knight mug bearing the printed mark, Registration applied for. Designed and modelled by Dame Laura Knight D.B.E., R.A., above the Royal Cypher of Edward VIII and the printed signature, Laura Knight. Shown with another unmarked mug with an enterprisingly modern handle. *Miss P.A. Burd Collection*

Dame Laura Knight's design is found on pieces bearing her printed mark and also on the wares of several potters including Wedgwood and Johnson Brothers of Hanley. It was widely adapted for George VI's Coronation.

86. Dame Laura Knight lion-head handle mug adapted for the Coronation of George VI. 3⅛″ h. *Harris Museum and Art Gallery, Preston*

106

87. & 88. Lidded loving cup in bone china for the Coronation of Edward
VIII. Produced by Wedgwood to the design of Dame Laura Knight. This
example is unfinished, presumably owing to the Abdication. The second
loving cup shows the design adapted for George VI. *Wedgwood*

89. Wedgwood mugs designed for the proposed Coronation of King Edward VIII. Left: mug in creamware by Keith Murray; right: mug in fine earthenware by Eric Ravilious. 4½″ h. and 4″ h. respectively. *Miss P.A. Burd Collection*

90. Wedgwood mug for the 1953 Coronation. A re-use of the Ravilious design made possible by the identical monograms of Edward and Elizabeth. 4″ h. *Wedgwood*

91. Jug in the form of the Coronation throne with the seated figure of Queen Elizabeth II. The base is printed with a history of the throne and a Coronation inscription. Marked Burleigh Ware, England. 7¼" h. *Private Collection*

92. Fine earthenware mug designed by Richard Guyatt as a Wedgwood Elizabeth commemorative. The shape of the mug is identical to that produced for Edward VIII and Elizabeth II bearing the Ravilious design. 4½" h. *Wedgwood*

Although at first sight the discreet elegance of the Wedgwood mug asserts itself as the finer of these two objects, the robust vulgarity of the jug is remarkably refreshing when compared with the stereotyped good taste of so many Coronation commemoratives.

93. Attempts to break away from traditional designs and add an element of modernity to Coronation commemoratives are rare. These four items, three of them are decidedly inexpensive, are examples of contemporary design. The Edward VII beaker shows the influence of the Arts and Crafts movement and is remarkably effective and simple; made by Minton, it measures $4\frac{1}{2}''$ high. The two George VI items reveal different aspects of Art Deco. The flask was produced for Emu Australian Wines, England, and the double handled jug is unmarked. The Elizabeth II stoneware mug was designed by Bernard Leach and produced by the Leach Pottery, St Ives. *Private Collection and Stoke and Leicester Museums*

94. George VI and Elizabeth II Coronation mugs bearing the official designs of the British Pottery Manufacturers' Federation. Pieces bearing these designs are stamped on the base with the Federations official mark. The George VI mug is 3½″ high and bears the mark of J. & G. Meakin; the Elizabeth mug measures 4″ and is stamped, Royal Harvey, Staffordshire. The production of an official design not only provided a service to Federation members but was also intended to maintain standards in the face of shoddy foreign imports. *Author's Collection*

95. The Mayor of Bilston, Staffordshire, presenting a Coronation mug bearing the official design. *Express and Star, Wolver–hampton*

96. The evolution of the Coronation mug, undoubtedly the most popular and enduring form of commemorative. In order from the top left to lower right: first period Worcester porcelain mug with Hancock's print of George III; William IV earthenware mug bearing, in addition to the Royal portraits, a Garter Star inscribed, *Reform*; Victoria Coronation mug attributed to Swansea; transferred and hand painted Edward VII mug by Frank Beardsmore, Fenton; George V mug signed M.E. Langfier and stamped Made in Germany; Edward VIII Staffordshire earthenware mug; Sutherland bone china George VI mug; Elizabeth II mug produced by The Coronation Pottery Co. *Private Collection*

97. Cut and engraved crystal bowl and a cut and engraved tankard designed for Edward VIII's Coronation by Stuart Crystal of Stourbridge. Stuarts produced seven other items for Edward's Coronation the majority of which did not leave the factory. *Photographs courtesy of Stuart Crystal Ltd.*

98. Cut and engraved crystal vase, 11″ high, weighing 9lbs, made by Stuart for George VI's Coronation. The mug is identical to that produced for Edward. *Photographs courtesy of Stuart Crystal Ltd.*

99. A press photograph showing Mr F.C. Shotton examining a footed chalice made by Webb Corbett Ltd and signed by the designer, Irene Stevens. *Express and Star, Wolverhampton.*

Most of the major crystal glass manufacturers produced items for Elizabeth II's Coronation. Limited editions are few although the majority of the finer items are signed and numbered. On the whole production of a particular design continued throughout the period during which use of the Royal Arms was granted by the Lord Chamberlain's office. The high cost of engraved glass tended to ensure that the more expensive items had a limited sale. Royal Brierley Crystal productions ranged in price from the limited edition Commonwealth Cup at £21 to the Great Britain Mug at 35s. engraved and 14s. etched. Many of the expensive items were also produced in technically cheaper ways.

100. Full lead crystal chalice, cut on the bowl with the Royal Arms and inscribed verso, *Elizabeth R. 1953*. Inscribed on the foot, *Long May She Reign*. Signed by the engraver, C.D. Smith and produced by Webb Corbett Ltd. Stourbridge. 11″ h. 6″ diam. *Webb Corbett Ltd.*

101. The Commonwealth Cup. Full lead crystal glass loving cup engraved with the Royal Arms and emblems of the Commonwealth countries. The base is marked, *The Commonwealth Cup. Royal Brierley Crystal.* Engraved by W.H. Cooke. 50 made. This is no. 47. 5″ h. 7½″ diam. *John Hoyle Esq.*

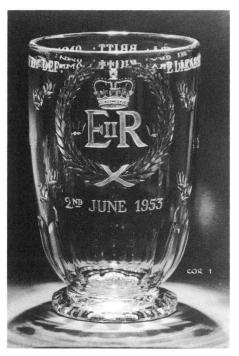

102. & 103. Glass produced for both the luxury and economy markets by Stuart Crystal in 1953. All four items were designed by John Luxton A.R.C.A. but whereas the tankard, tumbler and jug have etched cyphers, the vase is cut and engraved. The vase, 12″ high, was the first numbered limited edition made by Stuart, the edition was of one hundred. The cost of the vase in 1952 was £20, the jug cost 21s. the tankard 12s 6d and half a dozen tumblers 39s. *Stuart Crystal Ltd.*

104. *Left* Ashtray with pressed decoration of crown and inscription *Elizabeth R 1953*. 3″ diam. *Author's Collection*

Centre Blue enamelled glass transfer printed with the Royal Arms and the inscription, *Coronation of Queen Elizabeth II June 2nd 1953*. 4″ h. *Author's Collection*

Right Cruet in white glass on a gilt enamelled glass stand. Each piece transfer printed with the Royal Arms. 3″ max. h. *Wolverhampton Art Gallery and Museums*

Cheap glass items were produced for all the twentieth century Coronations. Transfer printing and moulding allowed for rapid inexpensive production.

105. & 106. Tumbler in pale red glass transferred in white with a bust portrait of King Edward VII and inscribed, *A Souvenir of the Coronation 26th June 1902*. 4″ h. *Wolverhampton Art Gallery and Museums*

107. & 108. Pressed and stamped tinware for twentieth century Coronations
The Metal Box Company Ltd.

Stamped and transferred tin containers were first produced in the late nineteenth century and thus are first found as Coronation souvenirs in 1902. The boxes were sold by the manufacturers to many confectionery and tobacco companies who, in turn, supplied many corporate bodies. They were an extremely popular public gift. Manchester alone issued 235,000 twopenny boxes of chocolates and 10,000 ninepenny boxes of tobacco or tea in 1911. Of the boxes shown the Edward VII tin was made for Rowntrees, the George VI and Elizabeth II boxes for Cadbury's, the money boxes for Oxo and the biscuit tins for Grey Dunn and Bulsland Bros. of Glasgow. The tray was one of the Metal Box Company's own souvenir items. The Metal Box Co. Ltd. was founded in 1921 as the result of the amalgamation of four old-established firms, Hudson Scott and Sons of Carlisle and Newcastle, Barclay Fry of Southwark and Portslade, F. Atkins and Co. of Hull and Henry Grant and Co. of South London.

109, 110 & 111. An unusual use of pressed tin to produce a commemorative free gift. This matchbox holder bears colour transfers of King George VI and Queen Elizabeth protected by a plastic film. The advertisers motto is appropriately loyal. $3\frac{1}{4}'' \times 2\frac{1}{2}'' \times \frac{3}{4}''$
Collection Gill Jackson

112. This silver beaker was given by the Marquess of Cholmondely, Joint Hereditary Chamberlain of England, to his page at the Coronation of King George VI. It is thus a personal memento. 4⅞″ h. *Private Collection*

Relatively few silver and gold items, other than medals, were produced before Elizabeth II's Coronation in 1953. The restrictions upon ownership of precious metals and the rise of the limited edition resulted in several Elizabethan commemoratives and the continuing trend towards speculation in gold and silver is shown by the many recent commemorative items in these metals.

113. Pewter items are naturally more plentiful than silver commemoratives. The majority take the form of tankards and many were no doubt extra-inscribed for births and comings of age. The example shown is a hand beaten sweetmeat dish with a silver medallion of Edward VIII in the centre. Manufactured by Marples, Wingfield and Wilkins of Sheffield in extremely small numbers. 5⅞″ diam. *Author's Collection*

114. Sterling silver sweetmeat dish. An extremely discreet souvenir with the 1953 Queen's Head Hallmark as the only Coronation emblem. 3″ diam. *Private Collection*

115. Contemporary model of the State Coach designed by Sir William Chambers and completed in 1762 at a total cost of £7,562 4s. 3d. *London Museum*

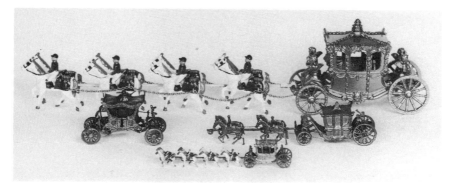

116. The four model coaches shown are: centre left, stamped gilt metal with red transparent windows, 2″ × 3″, a souvenir of the Coronation of George V; centre right, cast lead coach with four horses, 6″ long, George VI souvenir; foreground, silvered cast lead with enamel colours by Moko Toys, Lesney, 4¾″ long, for Elizabeth II's Coronation; background, gilded cast lead coach with eight hand coloured horses, Lesney Products and Co. Ltd., London, 15″ long, a souvenir of Elizabeth II's Coronation. *Private Collection*

Lead figures of George VI and Queen Elizabeth in their Coronation robes were manufactured by Britain's Ltd. of London.

117. A selection of cheap metal spoons, frequently used as gifts for schoolchildren. From left to right Edward VIII dessert spoon, 5″; George VI
teaspoon, E.P.N.S. by Mappin and Webb, 4½″, a gift from the West Riding
County Council; Elizabeth II stamped alloy caddy spoon, probably
supplied free with tea; Elizabeth II stamped alloy teaspoon, 4″; Elizabeth
II E.P.N.S. teaspoon, made in Sheffield, 4½″. *Author's Collection*

Silver spoons were also produced in large numbers. A particularly fine
set of six coffee spoons, each with the assay mark of a different office and
the 1953 Queen's Head stamp was produced in a numbered edition by
Joseph Gloster Ltd. of Birmingham.

118. Four horse brasses, Crown, Edward VII, George V and Elizabeth II.
Bedford Museum

Despite appearances the horse brass is a relatively modern phenomenon.
The commemorative ones shown are unlikely to have been intended for
harness decoration and are purely ornamental.

119. Cast and stamped brass bottle opener,
a gift from the soft drinks firm of Sherwood
and Morris as a souvenir of the 1953
Coronation. $5\frac{1}{4}''$. *Author's Collection*
A typical example of the cheap but relevant
souvenirs produced as free gifts by manufacturers.

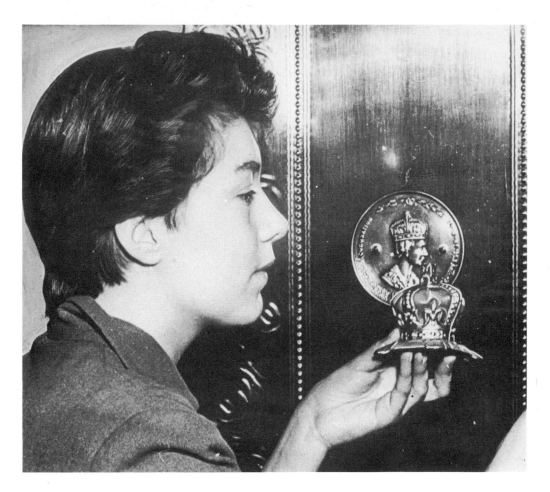

120. The Crown Money Box was produced in cast alloy by several firms in the Midlands and is found with either red and gold or blue, silver, red and gold decoration. Sizes vary from $3'' \times 3''$ to $3'' \times 3\frac{1}{2}''$. The caption to the press photograph reads, 'Miss Audrey Jones, a clerical worker in the office of a Walsall hardware manufacturer, gets a preview of a number of Coronation souvenirs, the latest being a money savings box in the shape of a Crown.' *Express and Star, Wolverhampton.*

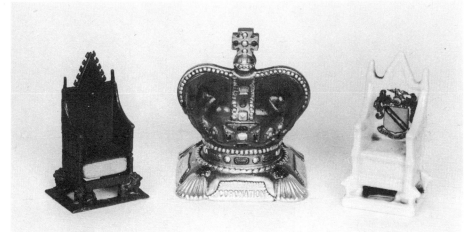

121. The two thrones are respectively a cast metal replica with a composition Stone of Scone incorporated below the seat produced as a souvenir for the Coronation of George V, $3\frac{1}{4}''$ h., and a porcelain version bearing Shakespeare's arms and lettered verso, W.H. Goss. Model of the Coronation Chair in Westminster Abbey. Rd. No. 578694. $3\frac{3}{8}''$ h. *Private Collection*

The Goss version was probably intended to be sold in Stratford on Avon, economically combining loyal and literary attributes.

122. Paper decoration or wall hanging to commemorate the Coronation of Edward VII. Colour lithograph, designed by W.Y. Calder from photographs by Gunn and Stuart of Richmond. 38½″ × 59″. *Whitworth Art Gallery, University of Manchester*

The production of large paper wall decorations of Royal subjects began in England in the nineteenth century. Victoria was the subject of a grisaille French paper of the 1840's and was commemorated in at least one Diamond Jubilee paper in 1897. Edward's Coronation Procession and Military Review were recorded on a paper also in the Whitworth. An Edward VII Coronation wallpaper was recently rediscovered on a wall at the Wheatsheaf Inn, Southwell, Nottinghamshire, which confirms the belief that the majority of Royal commemorative hangings and wall papers were intended for public gathering places rather than private houses.

123. Ticket to the Coronation of King George IV. Embossed and printed in blue and black. This ticket entitles the bearer to a seat in Poets' Corner and bears the signature of Lord Howard of Effingham, Deputy Earl Marshall. $8\frac{7}{8}'' \times 9\frac{7}{8}''$. *Bedford Museum*

124. Cigarette cards for the Coronations of George V and George VI. Both sets, one in a Souvenir Album, were produced by W.D. & H.O. Wills and each set contained fifty cards. The George V set are colour printed and show the Coronation Regalia and dignitaries. The George VI set are black and white photographic reproductions of incidents in the life of the new King. Cigarette firms had virtually ceased production of cards by 1953 but Typhoo Tea, among others, produced cards bearing 'Special Coronation Year Offers' on the reverse. *Wolverhampton Art Gallery and Museums*

125. Parasol. Paper with wooden handle and spokes. Marked, Empire Made. 20″ diam. *Wolverhampton Art Gallery and Museums*

Parasols were purchased by optimistic crowds attending Coronation celebrations throughout Britain; the actual day proved rainy. Plastic periscopes were another popular item among those attending the Procession. A more comfortable view of the ceremony could be obtained in the privacy of one's own home thanks to the medium of television. Films of the processions of Edward VII and George V were produced and the actual ceremony of George VI was filmed. The Coronations of George III and IV, William IV and Victoria were the subject of hand painted lantern slides.

126. & 127. Co-operative Society advertisement in the Birmingham Corporation Official Coronation Programme of 1911. *By courtesy of the Birmingham History Reference Library*

Commercial advertisements containing Coronation references first appear at the Coronation of Edward VII. The practice had reached saturation point by 1953 when every paper bag and wrapping bore loyal sentiments and the Express Dairy produced a milk bottle label which carried the Royal Cypher above the polite request, 'Would you please put your empty bottles out overnight in order to help our staff.' The principle charm of Coronation adverts lies in their incongruity.

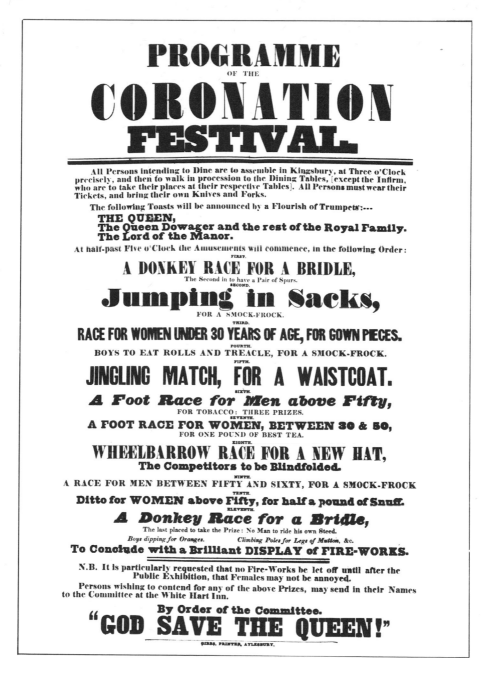

PROGRAMME
OF THE
CORONATION
FESTIVAL.

All Persons intending to Dine are to assemble in Kingsbury, at Three o'Clock precisely, and then to walk in procession to the Dining Tables, [except the Infirm, who are to take their places at their respective Tables]. All Persons must wear their Tickets, and bring their own Knives and Forks.

The following Toasts will be announced by a Flourish of Trumpets:—

THE QUEEN,
The Queen Dowager and the rest of the Royal Family.
The Lord of the Manor.

At half-past Five o'Clock the Amusements will commence, in the following Order:

FIRST.
A DONKEY RACE FOR A BRIDLE,
The Second in to have a Pair of Spurs.

SECOND.
Jumping in Sacks,
FOR A SMOCK-FROCK.

THIRD.
RACE FOR WOMEN UNDER 30 YEARS OF AGE, FOR GOWN PIECES.

FOURTH.
BOYS TO EAT ROLLS AND TREACLE, FOR A SMOCK-FROCK.

FIFTH.
JINGLING MATCH, FOR A WAISTCOAT.

SIXTH.
A Foot Race for Men above Fifty,
FOR TOBACCO: THREE PRIZES.

SEVENTH.
A FOOT RACE FOR WOMEN, BETWEEN 30 & 50,
FOR ONE POUND OF BEST TEA.

EIGHTH.
WHEELBARROW RACE FOR A NEW HAT,
The Competitors to be Blindfolded.

NINTH.
A RACE FOR MEN BETWEEN FIFTY AND SIXTY, FOR A SMOCK-FROCK

TENTH.
Ditto for WOMEN above Fifty, for half a pound of Snuff.

ELEVENTH.
A Donkey Race for a Bridle,
The last placed to take the Prize: No Man to ride his own Steed.

Boys dipping for Oranges.   *Climbing Poles for Legs of Mutton, &c.*
To Conclude with a Brilliant DISPLAY of FIRE-WORKS.

N.B. It is particularly requested that no Fire-Works be let off until after the Public Exhibition, that Females may not be annoyed.

Persons wishing to contend for any of the above Prizes, may send in their Names to the Committee at the White Hart Inn.

By Order of the Committee.
"GOD SAVE THE QUEEN!"

GIBBS, PRINTER, AYLESBURY.

by courtesy of the Buckinghamshire County Museum Service

128. & 129. *Left* Petersham ribbon transfer printed in black and hand coloured in purple, green, red and yellow. The design incorporates St Edward's Crown, the Garter Star and the Prince of Wales' Feathers. A souvenir of the Coronation of King George IV. Similar examples are in the Victoria and Albert Museum. 2½″ wide. *Wolverhampton Art Gallery and Museums*

Right Rayon tie, produced as a souvenir for the Coronation of Edward VIII. Four designs were produced each incorporating crowns, royal cyphers etc. This tie bears the label, 'Greville Reg'd.' A singularly appropriate souvenir given the sartorial fame of the King and his subsequent invention of the 'Windsor' knot. *Wolverhampton Art Gallery and Museums*

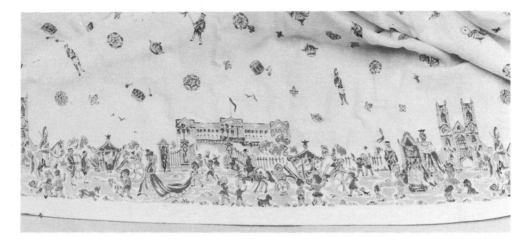

130. Cotton fabric, colour printed with Royal emblems and a child's version of the Coronation ceremony and procession. Produced in 1953. *Private Collection*

Apart from the many commercially produced fabric designs, recent Coronations have all been commemorated by items incorporating the fabrics used for the Coronation Robes of monarchs and peers. They vary from the simple 'Coronation Velvet Butterfly' made from the same 'All British Purple Silk Velvet used for the Coronation Robes of George VI and Queen Elizabeth', made by Reville of London, to a sumptuous limited edition book. *British Traditional Colours* was produced as a George VI souvenir by the British Colour Council. The 250 copies of the Edition de Luxe were each signed by the Earl of Derby and contain fifty original fabrics, including the ribbons of the Orders of Knighthood and the actual material to be used in the making of the Coronation Robes of the King, Queen, Duchesses of Gloucester and Kent, Peers and Peeresses. The demand for authentic Coronation objects also led to the sale of the chairs and stools used by the Coronation congregation. Offered originally to those who used them they were available to the general public by 1953. This practice is a purely twentieth century one.

Many small favours and souvenirs were woven from Coventry and Macclesfield silk. Thomas Stevens of Coventry produced items for the Coronations of Edward VII, George V and George VI, the last adapted from the design for Edward VIII. W.H. Grant of Coventry made souvenirs for all the Coronations from Edward VII to Elizabeth II and Brocklehursts of Macclesfield issued a large design for Elizabeth II.

131. & 132. The two press photographs from the Wolverhampton Express and Star show '*Albion St., Willenhall, one of the best decorated streets*' and the '*Coronation beacon being built at Heath Hayes which is expected to be one of the largest fires in the country. It is 40 ft. high.*'

Many towns held competitions for the best decorated streets and official plaques were presented to the winners. Civic rejoicing took both ephemeral and permanent forms. Roads built or adapted by public corporations in 1902, 1911, 1937 and 1953 were quite likely to be named Coronation Street or Coronation Road. Almost every town in England has one. Birmingham boasts two Coronation Roads, both christened in 1902. A less urban manifestation was the planting of trees and the naming of parks and playgrounds. Trees were planted in the majority of English boroughs, those in Liverpool for 1937 were planted by the Mayor, Mayoress, Dean, Choir Boy and Chief Cadet. Both 1937 and 1953 saw Coronation planting schemes. The extent of the planting for George VI's Coronation is detailed in a book with the resounding title *The Royal Record of Tree Planting, the Provision of Open Spaces, Recreation Grounds and Other Schemes Undertaken in the British Empire and Elsewhere, Especially in the United States of America in Honour of the Coronation of His Gracious Majesty King George VI* compiled by R.G. Gordon and produced by the Coronation Planting Committee in 1939. The growth of the planting of trees coincided with the decline in the erection of Royal statues, which, during the nineteenth century, were erected at the beginning of a reign (five are recorded in Gunnis[32] within two years of George IV's Coronation and four each for William and Victoria) and in the twentieth century assume a memorial function.

Bibliography

A book such as this, necessarily covering a wide range of specialised subjects, is compounded of the fruits of one's own research and the crumbs from other men's tables. It would be impossible to list all the books I have read in the course of research but those listed below have either supplied me with material for major themes or specialised items.

GENERAL

LAWRENCE TANNER, *The History of the Coronation*, New York, 1953.
The Connoisseur Coronation Book, edited by L. G. Ramsay, 1953.
Apollo Coronation Number, June 1953.
JAMES MACKAY, *Commemorative Pottery and Porcelain*, Garnstone Press, 1971.
JOHN and JENNIFER MAY, *Commemorative Pottery 1780–1900,* Heinemann, 1972.
Wolverhampton Art Gallery, *A Health Unto Their Majesties,* 1973.

MEDALS

JAMES MACKAY, *Commemorative Medals*, Barker, 1970.
J. R. S. WHITING, *Commemorative Medals*, David and Charles, 1972.
JOSEPH EDMUNDSON, *Collecting Modern Commemorative Medals*, Pelham, 1972.

DELFT

ANTHONY RAY, *English Delftware in the Robert Hall Warren Collection*, Faber and Faber, 1972.
F. H. GARNER and MICHAEL ARCHER, *English Delftware*, Faber and Faber, 1972.

SLIPWARE

RONALD COOPER, *English Slipware Dishes 1650–1850,* Tiranti, 1968.

GLASS

JOSEPH BLES, *Rare English Glasses of the 17th and 18th Centuries,* private printing, 1925.

Arthur Churchill Ltd., *History in Glass,* 1937.

W. A. THORPE, *English Glass,* A. & C. Black, 1961.

E. M. ELVILLE, *The Collector's Dictionary of Glass,* Country Life, 1967.

PORCELAIN and POTTERY

CYRIL COOK, *The Life and Work of Robert Hancock and Supplement,* Chapman and Hall, 1948.

BERNARD WATNEY, *English Blue and White Porcelain of the 18th Century,* Faber and Faber, 1963.

GEOFFREY GODDEN, *English Pottery and Porcelain 1780–1850,* Barker, 1963.

GEOFFREY GODDEN, *Illustrated Encyclopaedia of English Pottery and Porcelain,* Barrie and Jenkins, 1970.

GRISELDA LEWIS, *A Collector's History of English Pottery,* Studio Vista, 1969.

MONOGRAPHS

ALICE K. EARLY, *English Dolls, Effigies and Puppets,* Batsford, 1955.

P. D. GORDON PUGH, *Staffordshire Portrait Figures,* Barrie and Jenkins, 1970.

GEOFFREY GODDEN, *Stevengraphs,* Barrie and Jenkins, 1971.

CYRIL WILLIAMS-WOOD, *Staffordshire Pot Lids and their Potters,* Faber and Faber, 1972.

LINDA HANNAS, *The English Jig Saw Puzzle 1760–1890,* Wayland, 1972.

ROBIN REILLY and GEORGE SAVAGE, *Wedgwood Portrait Medallions,* Barrie and Jenkins, 1973.

MARY S. MORRIS, *English 18th and 19th Century Enamels in the Wolverhampton and Bilston Collections,* Wolverhampton Art Gallery, 1973.

Index

The references in **bold type** are to the captions to the illustrations.